BIRTHDAY PARTIES FOR KIDS!

Creative Party Ideas
Your Kids and Their Friends Will Love

Penny Warner

Prima Publishing

To Rebecca, Matthew, and Tom

Published by Prima Publishing, Roseville, California. Member of the Crown Publishing Group, a division of Random House, Inc., New York.

Library of Congress Cataloging-in-Publication Data
Warner, Penny.
   Birthday parties for kids! : creative party ideas your kids and their friends will love / Penny Warner.
     p.   cm.
   Includes index.
   ISBN 0-7615-0125-8, 0-7615-1450-3
   1. Children's parties.   2. Birthdays.   I. Title.
  GV1205.W376   1995
  793.2'1—dc20   95-31380
                                          CIP

02 03 04 05 II 10 9 8 7 6
Printed in the United States of America
First Edition

Visit us online at www.primapublishing.com

CONTENTS

INTRODUCTION   1

Twelve Steps to Perfect Party Planning
Plan a Theme for the Party
Plan the Party with Your Child
Plan the Time and Keep It Short
Plan the Guest List
Plan the Decorations to Suit the Theme
Plan the Games and Activities
Plan the Goodies
Plan the Prizes for Both Winners
    and Losers
Plan for Surprises
Plan for Problems
Plan for Fun
Plan for Yourself!

BIRTHDAY PARTY THEMES   9

Arts and Crafts Party
Backyard Camp Party

Balloon Blow-Out Party
Beach Party
Bedtime Party
Big & Little Party
Bookworm Party
Bouncy Baby Party
Cartoony Party
Cheerleading Party
Chefs in the Kitchen Party
Chocolate Candy Land Party
Clown-Around Party
Come-as-You-Are Party
Cookie Party
Creepy Critter Party
Daily Planet Party
Dancing with a DJ Party
Doll and Action Figure Party
Fashion Victim Party
Freaky Friday Party
Game Show Party
Gilligan's Island Party

Gold Medal Games Party
Great White Shark Party
Grow Up! Party
Haunted House Party
Hippie Sixties Party
Hooray for Hollywood Party
Horsin' Around Party
Jurassic Party
Magical Party
Mommy and Daddy Party
Mother Goose Party
Movie-Making Party
Musical Party
Mystery Mansion Party
Pajama Party
Pet Party
Photo Party
Pirate Party
Punk Party
Puzzle Party
Restaurant Party
Salon Style Party
Scary Monster Party
Scientific Expedition Party

Sci-Fi Party
Sdrawkcab Party
Secret Spy Party
Sherwood forest Party
Skaters and Bikers Party
Sock Hop
South of the Border Party
Space Trek Party
Storytime Party
Summer in Winter or Winter in
    Summer Party
Sunrise Surprise Party
Superheroes Party
Talent Show Party
Teddy Bear Picnic
This Is Your Life Party
Trains, Planes, and Automobiles Party
Tropical Luau
Under the Sea Party
Video Game Party
Water World Party
Where in the World . . . Party
Zoo Party

GREAT KID GAMES   117

FUN PARTY FOODS 185

Super Snacks
All-You-Can-Eat Buffet
Banana Butter Buns
Colossal Cookie
Mixin' Munchies
Painted Cookies
Potato Puffers
Puffy People
Silly Sailboats
Stuffed Bananas

Dazzling Drinks
Children's Champagne
Chocolate Fizz
Glow Drink
Hawaiian Hurricane
Milk 'n' Cookies Shake
Monkey Milkshake
Peanut Butter Blitz
Straw Sucker

Mini-Meals
Bread Bowler
Brunch-on-a-Stick

Elephant Eggs
Jell-O Crunch
Porcupine Pat
Quicksand Dip
Shape Sandwiches

Creative Cakes
Blackbeard's Treasure
Carousel Cake
Clown Cakes
Crazy Cupcakes
Dressy Doll Cake
Hamburger Cake
Meteor Shower Cake
Surprise-Inside Cake

Ice Cream Dreams
Chocolate Pasta Ice Cream
Crispy Crunch Ice Cream Pie
Coffee Can Ice Cream
Dirt and Worms
Ice Cream Clowns
Igloos
Orange Oddballs
Spider Web Pie

ACKNOWLEDGMENTS

Many, many thanks to the following families, friends, teachers, parents, and students at Diablo Valley College, Chabot College, and Ohlone College, for contributing their wonderful ideas:

Charlie Ahern, Chad Anderson, Linda Barde, Jennifer Basye, Deya Brashears, Barbara Burri, Victor Chen, Craig Clemetson, Jason Cosetti, Jonathan Ellington, Melanie Ellington, Steven Ellington, Bob Goll, Dave Goll, Deborah Gohlke, Brian Hurley, Jonnie Jacobs, Peggy Lucke, Lynn MacDonald, Norma Meyerholtz, Wende Music, Peyton Nattinger, Stacey Norris, Connie Pike, Ed Pike, Geoffrey Pike, Melody Pike, Sally Richards, Brie Saunders, Brooke Saunders, Chris Saunders, Kelli Saunders, Kristin Saunders, Sean Saunders, Barbara Swec, Jana Swec, Joseph Swec, Len Swec, Tim Swec, Sunanda Rao, Frank Ruiz, Jim Russell, Shahla Saudaguran, Kimberly Saunders, Jill Seavey, Susan Stadelhofer, Vicki Stadelhofer, Mia Thiele, Heather Thornton, Sheila Timmons, Holly Valdez, Samuel Valdez, Zachary Valdez, Alex Warner, Doreen Warner, Terry Warner, Mary Warner, Nick Warner, Simonie Webster, and Dakota Webster.

A very special thanks to my editor, Alice Anderson, and my agent, Lyle Steele.

INTRODUCTION

Birthdays are so special to children, full of magic and surprises. They're especially exciting when enhanced with guests, gifts, games, and cake and ice cream, too.

Hosting a happy birthday party for your child doesn't have to be a hassle. It can be a "piece of cake"—with a little help from the themes, ideas, suggestions, and tips provided in *Birthday Parties for Kids!* We'll help you take care of everything, from the welcoming invitations to the good-bye favors, all in the following pages.

Birthday Parties for Kids! is full of creative mix-and-match suggestions for unique homemade celebrations. All you have to do is flip through the seven chapters to find your favorite ideas, then follow the instructions and watch how easily they come to life.

Simply choose a theme, pick out related invitations, create decorations, organize the games and activities, prepare the fun-to-eat food, and select the favors that match your party festivities. With a little imagination and some suggestions from the book, the party possibilities and combinations are endless! And they're quick, easy, and inexpensive, too!

Before you begin, read over the Twelve Steps to Perfect Party Planning to help make your special occasion a guaranteed success.

TWELVE STEPS TO PERFECT PARTY PLANNING

PLAN A THEME FOR THE PARTY

A theme offers a focus for the invitations, decorations, games, activities, food, and favors, and helps the party fall into place. Organize the party around your child's particular interests. Or ask what he or she would like to celebrate at the birthday party, and make everything related to that subject. If you need suggestions, consider the following: your child's favorite toy or doll, a special movie or television show, a sports figure or the sport itself, a current movie or movie star, a popular song or rock star, a storybook or cartoon character, a superhero or monster, a game or activity, a favorite location or outing, a popular hometown hero or local star, an interesting occupation or hobby, a special food or festival, or a holiday or event.

Special Tip: If your child has trouble choosing a theme, notice what he or she is currently playing with or enjoying. Then surprise your child with a birthday party centered on that special character, interest, or activity.

PLAN THE PARTY WITH YOUR CHILD

Let your child help with the party plans to keep him or her busy during the days or weeks before the special event. That way your child will be actively involved in the creation of the party, which is almost as fun as the party itself. Have him or her help make the invitations, decorate the party room, plan the games, organize the activities, prepare the fun foods, and create or choose the favors that go home with the party guests. Engaging your child in the party planning makes the birthday celebration last longer and helps him or her manage the excitement and anticipation.

Special Tip: Make the week prior to the party a celebration in itself by completing one special party-related activity each day until the big event.

PLAN THE TIME AND KEEP IT SHORT

A well-planned party begins and ends at specific times and doesn't run too long or too short. Two hours in the morning or afternoon is best, depending on your child's energy level, so think about whether your child does better in the morning or afternoon, and plan the party accordingly. Hosting a party for a two-hour period allows time for welcoming the guests, playing a number of games and activities, opening presents, sharing refreshments and cake, and saying farewells.

Special Tip: Be sure to remind the parents of the exact time the party ends. Your guests usually will have had enough excitement for one day. Also, your child will need some peace and quiet after all the festivities, and time to enjoy the gifts and memories of the party.

PLAN THE GUEST LIST

Have your child plan the guest list with you and encourage limiting invitations to good friends only. That way you can manage the party size.

If you prefer a large group, ask a few of the parents to help out during the party to keep things under control. Also decide whether relatives will be invited, if adults will be included or just kids, and especially how to involve siblings in the preparations and event.

Special Tip: If parents can't help out, hire baby-sitters or neighborhood teenagers to assist you during the celebration. The more hands you have to help out, the easier your party will be.

PLAN THE DECORATIONS TO SUIT THE THEME

First decide where you'll be hosting the party— indoors or out. Let the weather be your guide, making sure you can adapt your activities to indoor or outdoor play at the last minute. Be sure you have enough room for your guests and that no valuable breakables are in the area. Decorate the party room or yard to suit the theme. Create a backdrop that sets the mood by using poster board, construction paper, crepe paper, balloons, special lighting, and appropri-ate music. Give the birthday kid a crown, a cape, a make-over, a new outfit, a certificate of achievement, a distinctive place setting, or a special toy or prop.

Special Tip: Let the guest of honor help out with creating the decorations. It helps keep the child busy and involved in the upcoming celebration. Create lots of do-it-yourself dec-orations rather than use store-bought ones to make the party more personal. Close areas of the house or yard that are off limits, and remove anything in the party area that is dan-gerous, breakable, or valuable. Also remove any of your child's toys that he or she does not want to share with the guests.

PLAN THE GAMES AND ACTIVITIES

A perfect party offers both quiet activities and vigorous games. This allows the guests to warm up slowly, release pent-up energy, then cool down at the end of the party. If they don't know each other well, start out with a gentle introductory game. Play a few active games— preferably outside—after they have relaxed and become comfortable. Then settle down with a quiet game or activity in preparation for the cake and ice cream, and opening of the gifts.

Special Tip: You can never have too many games or activities, but you can have too few—and that can be disastrous. Be sure you plan more games and activities than you think you need, in case the kids run through them quickly, or the party goes overtime. Celebrations often turn to chaos when there's not enough to keep energetic kids busy. Keep a collection of art materials or boxed games nearby to bring out when there's nothing left to do.

PLAN THE GOODIES

Cake and ice cream are usually the highlight of the party, but you may want to limit sweets and provide some healthy snacks or meals so the guests won't overload on junk food. Have some handy treats around for the hungry snackers, but make them low in sugar and high in nutrition, such as cheese and crackers, pieces of fruit, nuts, raisins, or cut-up veggies. If you pre-fer to serve a more nutritious cake than the usual variety, try angel food or carrot cake topped with fruit, jam, or softened frozen yogurt.

Special Tip: Check out the Fun Party Foods chapter for fun-to-make and fun-to-eat party treats. You'll find everything from drinks and snacks to creative kids' meals to birthday cakes and ice cream concoctions. Decorate the cake to suit your theme, using creative shapes, fancy frosting, and little plastic toys to give it personality.

PLAN PRIZES FOR BOTH WINNERS AND LOSERS

Losing a game can take away the fun for some of the guests at your party, so don't overemphasize winning, especially with younger kids. Losing often leads to disappointment, frustration, and tears. If your older party guests appreciate competition, offer a few games that allow them to challenge one another, with group winners instead of individual winners. And try to offer enough games to give everyone a chance to win.

Special Tip: Every time someone loses, offer a funny booby prize, such as a rubber snake, oversized underwear, or a silly hat, so the guest doesn't feel bad about losing and still feels like a winner.

PLAN FOR SURPRISES

Anything can happen at a child's birthday party, so keep the cameras handy, both video and still, and record the fun to play back at the end of the party or after the guests have gone home. If the party games or activities don't go according to plan, just go with the flow. Sometimes the spontaneous happenings are the most fun!

Special Tip: If possible, take Polaroid snapshots of each guest to hand out to them as they leave so they have a memento of the party fun.

PLAN FOR PROBLEMS

Stuff happens, especially at birthday parties. If you expect things to go wrong now and then, you won't be surprised when they do. Keep your sense of humor and try to adjust to the unexpected. If the kids don't enjoy a game, or refuse a food, or won't participate in the fun, be creative and make some suitable changes that please everyone. If siblings have trouble with the birthday festivities, involve them in the party planning so they can feel a part of the fun. Have them invite a friend to the party to play with. Give them something special to do at the party to help out and make them feel important. And give them a thank-you gift before or after the party to let them know you appreciate their help.

Special Tip: Watch for the child who doesn't seem to fit in. Extra attention and special guidance can help him or her enjoy the party too.

PLAN FOR FUN

Remember the purpose of all this planning is a happy birthday party! Sometimes the guest of honor becomes overwhelmed with all the attention received on this special occasion. Try to give your child time to relax, and relieve the stress of all the excitement by planning a few quiet activities or distractions before and after the party. Understand and acknowledge your child's moods and feelings, and help your child find positive ways to enjoy this very exciting day. Sometimes the pressure and attention can get to be too much, so give your child a break in the middle of the party, if necessary, by having him or her help serve the food, set up a game, or do a special task.

Special Tip: Be sure your child has a proper meal and a rest or quiet time before the party begins. Encourage your child to talk about all the feelings that are bubbling up.

PLAN FOR YOURSELF!

Since you're the one doing most of the work, treat yourself to a bath, a quiet moment, or a special activity before or after the party to help you enjoy the festivities as well. Then pat yourself on the back for a well-planned, creative, and one-of-a-kind party that your child will remember for years to come.

Special Tip: If you plan everything ahead of time, the party will surely be a piece of cake!

BIRTHDAY PARTY THEMES

The best birthday parties begin with a theme. A specific theme helps give the celebration a focus, and it stimulates ideas for the flavor of the party, from the opening invitations to the farewell favors.

You can ask your child to pick a favorite toy, character, sport, or event to use as a theme, or choose a theme based on your child's current interests.

Or if you have trouble coming up with ideas, simply select a theme from the suggestions below. You can change the names, shapes, colors, or any other aspect of the suggestions to coordinate with everything else at your party.

You might want to feature an event, such as a mini-circus or magic show. Or "go Hollywood" and design the party around a movie, such as a Disney cartoon or favorite action film. If there is a special activity that your child enjoys—like playing soccer, reading mystery stories, or taking photographs—make that your central focus and design the party around it. Your theme might include an outing to a baseball game, beauty salon, zoo, or other interesting location. Or you might want to have a special guest come to entertain the kids, such as a firefighter, magician, artist, or other creative person.

Once you have your theme, use your imagination to create theme-related invitations, decorations, games, activities, food, and favors that coordinate with your child's taste and personality. Or refer to the individual chapters of this book for specific ideas to complete your party, adapting them as needed to fit the theme. For example, use the Cookie-on-a-Stick invitation for any number of parties, by shaping the cookie into an animal, a heart, a star, or a balloon.

Decorate the party room with Billions of Balloons for a background at your Hooray for Hollywood Party, This Is Your Life Party, Clown-Around Party, or Under the Sea Party.

Adapt the Funny Fashion Show Relay for any party that requires a costume or outfit, such as the Bouncy Baby Party, Sherwood Forest Party, Sock Hop, or Gilligan's Island Party. With a little imagination, the Face Painting activity could be fun at a Salon Style Party, a Hippie Sixties Party, a Punk Party, or a Zoo Party.

Rename the food suggestions listed in the Fun Party Foods chapter and watch the All-You-Can-Eat Buffet become a Take-a-Taco Bar, a

Select-a-Sandwich Deli, a Decorate-Your-Cake Shop, or a Mystery-Meal Menu.

Finally, offer favors that coordinate with the festivities, such as Bubble Stuff for the Scientific Expedition Party, the Arts and Crafts Party, the Balloon Blow-Out Party, or the Clown-Around Party.

ARTS AND CRAFTS PARTY

Welcome the future Picassos, Warhols, and Michelangelos to your Arts and Crafts Party. You provide the art supplies, and the budding artists will do the rest. Be sure to have lots of smocks and rags handy. These creative types can really make a mess!

Invitations: Balloon Blimps, Bubble Fun, Floral Fantasies, Popper Invitations, Pop-Up Cards, Puzzler Invitations, Swirl Stick Invitations.

Decorations: Artist Colony, Billions of Balloons, Comic-Cartoon Town.

Games: Black-Out, Funny Fashion Show Relay, Goofy Face, Picture Puzzle.

Activities: Creative Construction, Face It!, Face Painting, Fashion Fun, Finger Funnies, Funny Face, Gooshy Goo, Photo Paper Dolls, Salt Scape, Sixties Shirts.

Food: Painted Cookies, Puffy People, Straw Sucker, Porcupine Pat, Shape Sandwiches, Crazy Cupcakes, Surprise-Inside Cake, Dirt and Worms, Ice Cream Clowns.

Favors: Art Box, Baker's Clay Jewelry, Baker's Clay Picture Frames, Bubble Stuff, Edible Jewelry, Face Paints, Makeup Set, Puzzler Invitations, Surprise Balls, Weird Candy.

BACKYARD CAMP PARTY

You don't need a forest or a mountain for a camp-out party. You can host an outdoor overnighter right in your own backyard. Have the kids bring camping equipment, such as sleeping bags and flashlights, along with comic books to share while you pitch the tent, start the barbecue, and prepare a few ghost stories.

Invitations: Color Comics, Floral Fantasies, Garden Grow, Glow-in-the-Dark Star Chart, Picture Postcards, Pirate's Map, Ticket to Fun.

Decorations: Casbah Canopy, Enchanted Forest, Mystery Mansion, Spider's Den, Spooky Cave, Starry Starry Night, Tent Safari, Treasure Island.

Games: Bomb Squad, Boogie Man, Cocoon, Detective, Follow the Footprints, Go Fishing, Hot Lava, Oddball Olympics, Poison!, Quicksand, Tail Tag, Treasure Hunt, Water Balloon Blast-Off, Water Brigade, Winker.

Activities: Black Hole, Blind Walk, Chocolate Critters, Comic Strips, Dinosaur Egg Hunt, Galaxy Gazers, Ghosts and Goblins, Hairy Head, Pipeline, Popcorn Explosion, Salt Scape, Stork Walkers.

Food: All-You-Can-Eat Buffet, Glow Drink, Hawaiian Hurricane, Monkey Milkshake, Brunch-on-a-Stick, Elephant Eggs, Porcupine Pat, Quicksand Dip, Blackbeard's Treasure, Hamburger Cake, Meteor Shower Cake, Coffee Can Ice Cream, Dirt and Worms, Spider Web Pie.

Favors: Ants-in-the-Sand, Beach Finds, Boats and Floaters, Bug Collection, Coconut Heads, Comic Books, Compass and Treasure Map, Dinosaur Zoo, Freaky Frisbees, Gold Coins and Funny Money, Pirate Loot, Rubber Buggies, Secret Stash Trail Mix, Squirt Toys, Toothbrush-to-Go, Water Fun, Whistles and Tweeters.

BALLOON BLOW-OUT PARTY

Most party planners use balloons to liven up the festivities. But why not have a whole birthday party based on the symbol of happy parties—balloons!—with balloon invitations, decorations, and favors. Then, play lots of balloon games to inflate the fun!

Invitations: Balloon Blimps, Cookie-on-a-Stick, Egg-Citing Invitations, Mystery Messages, Pogs, Pop-Up Cards.

Decorations: Billions of Balloons, Carnival Booths, Casbah Canopy, Speech Balloons.

Games: Balloon Bodybuilder, Bomb Squad, Bumbling Bubble Gum, Oddball Olympics, Step 'n' Pop, Water Balloon Blast-Off.

Activities: Bubble Machine, Creative Construction, Dinosaur Egg Hunt, Gooshy Goo, Marble Mania, Popcorn Explosion, Surprise Bags.

Food: Colossal Cookie, Painted Cookies, Potato Puffers, Bread Bowler, Elephant Eggs, Porcupine Pat, Shape Sandwiches, Clown Cakes, Meteor Shower Cake, Ice Cream Clowns, Igloos, Orange Oddballs.

Favors: Bubble Stuff, Coconut Heads, Personalized Popcorn Balls, Surprise Balls.

BEACH PARTY

Here's the perfect party if you live near a beach. You also can turn your backyard into a mini-beach with a little creativity. Slap on the suntan lotion, grab the beach towels, fill the sandbox, switch on the Hawaiian music, hang up some colorful paper fish, and open the beach umbrellas—it's time for a fun-in-the-sun Beach Party!

Invitations: Bubble Fun, Picture Postcards, Ticket to Fun.

Decorations: Billions of Balloons, Casbah Canopy, Hawaiian Island, Parallel Universe, Sunny Day, Tent Safari, Treasure Island, Where in the World . . . .

Games: Body Bingo, Bomb Squad, Do-It Dice, Follow the Footprints, Giggle-Gut, Go Fishing,

Goose Feathers, Hot Lava, Oddball Olympics, Poison!, Quicksand, Step 'n' Pop, Tail Tag, Treasure Hunt, Water Balloon Blast-Off, Water Brigade.

Activities: Blind Walk, Bubble Machine, Candy Leis, Dinosaur Egg Hunt, Hairy Head, Pipeline, Salt Scape, Stork Walkers.

Food: Mixin' Munchies, Silly Sailboats, Hawaiian Hurricane, Quicksand Dip, Blackbeard's Treasure, Hamburger Cake, Meteor Shower Cake, Dirt and Worms, Igloos.

Favors: Ants-in-the-Sand, Beach Finds, Boats and Floaters, Bubble Stuff, Bug Collection, Compass and Treasure Map, Dinosaur Zoo, Freaky Frisbees, Pirate Loot, Rubber Buggies, Secret Stash Trail Mix, Squirt Toys, Water Fun, Whistles and Tweeters.

BEDTIME PARTY

Most kids don't like bedtime. It means missing all the fun—unless bedtime means party time! Invite the insomniacs over in their pajamas for a slumber party that's guaranteed to make everyone drowsy—by morning!

Invitations: Come-as-You-Are, Cookie-on-a-Stick, Glow-in-the-Dark Star Chart, This Is Your Life.

Decorations: Baby Love, Candy Land, Casbah Canopy, Disneyroom, Mystery Mansion, Starry, Starry Starry Night.

Games: A-B-C Game, Body Bingo, Boogie Man, Broken Mirror, Candy Grab, Candy Wrap, Commercial Crazy, Crime Scene, Detective, Dictionary, Do-It Dice, Funny Fashion Show Relay, Giggle-Gut, Goofy Face, Heart Surgeon, Hoppin' Hats, Mind Reader, Mortuary, Name the Tune, Pass the Present, Picture Puzzle, Poison!, Prize Is Right, Screen Test, Shoe Loose, Snap—or Zap!, Sound Stage, Taster's Tongue, Thief!, Winker.

Activities: Amazing Swami, Black Hole, Candy Leis, Face It! Face Painting, Fashion Fun, Finger Funnies, Funny Face, Galaxy Gazers, Ghosts and Goblins, Hansel and Gretel's House, Model Behavior, Mysterious Message, Photo Paper Dolls, Popcorn Explosion, Sixties Shirts, Storybook Theater, Super Stickers, Surprise Bags, Treasure or Trash?

Food: All-You-Can-Eat Buffet, Banana Butter Buns, Stuffed Bananas, Children's Champagne, Glow Drink, Milk 'n' Cookies Shake, Brunch-on-a-Stick, Jell-O Crunch, Crazy Cupcakes, Dressy Doll Cake, Hamburger Cake, Surprise-Inside Cake, Coffee Can Ice Cream, Orange Oddballs.

Favors: Baker's Clay Jewelry, Baker's Clay Picture Frames, Bunch of Books, Capes and Hats, Color Shapes, Comic Books, Edible Jewelry, Face Paints, Fake Tattoos and Earrings, False Fingernails, Faux Jewelry, Makeup Set, Me Doll, Pasta Necklaces, Poppers, Single Cassettes, Star Cards, Surprise Balls, Swirl Sticks, Thrift Store Ensembles, Toothbrush-to-Go, Weird Candy, White Elephant Gifts.

BIG & LITTLE PARTY

For an adventure down Alice's rabbit hole, host a Big & Little Party, where everything is either giant size or miniature—or a combination of both. Use large cardboard boxes to create the big stuff, and doll accessories for the small stuff. Or cut out decorations from construction paper in teeny-tiny and/or oversized shapes.

Invitations: Balloon Blimps, Crazy Invitations, Cut-Out Kids, Masquerade Disguises, Mystery Messages, Puzzler Invitations, Swirl Stick Invitations, This Is Your Life.

Decorations: All About You, Baby Love, Big & Little, Candy Land, Disneyroom, Footprints, Mystery Mansion, Parallel Universe, Where in the World . . . .

Games: Balloon Bodybuilder, Black-Out, Body Bingo, Broken Mirror, Bumbling Bubble Gum, Do-It Dice, Follow the Footprints, Funny Fashion Show Relay, Giant's Game, Mortuary, Oddball Olympics, Picture Puzzle, Treasure Hunt.

Activities: Blind Walk, Box Cars, Chocolate Critters, Dinosaur Egg Hunt, Face Painting, Fashion Fun, Hairy Head, Hansel and Gretel's House, Photo Paper Dolls, Stork Walkers, Storybook Theater.

Food: Colossal Cookie, Puffy People, Bread Bowler, Elephant Eggs, Dressy Doll Cake, Hamburger Cake, Ice Cream Clowns, Igloos.

Favors: Awards and Ribbons, Baker's Clay Jewelry, Bug Collection, Capes and Hats, Coconut Heads, Dinosaur Zoo, Magnetic Monsters, Me Doll, Rabbit-in-a-Hat, Rubber Buggies, Weird Candy, White Elephant Gifts.

BOOKWORM PARTY

A Bookworm Party isn't just for book lovers. Everyone has fun when a favorite book comes alive. Set the stage with a room full of children's literature and you're on your way to Oz, Green Gables, or Never-Never Land. You can gather a collection of popular books from the library, ask the guests to bring a well-loved book, choose one book for the party theme, or create giant book covers from poster board and paint, featuring real book titles, or made-up titles using the guests' names.

Invitations: Book-a-Party, Color Comics, Cut-Out Kids, Masquerade Disguises, Mystery Messages, Picture Postcards, Pop-Up Cards, Puzzler Invitations.

Decorations: Blast to the Past, Candy Land, Comic-Cartoon Town, Disneyroom, Enchanted Forest, Parallel Universe, Speech Balloons.

Games: Bumbling Bubble Gum, Cocoon, Commercial Crazy, Dictionary, Funny Fashion Show Relay, Giant's Game, Goofy Face, Hoppin' Hats, Picture Puzzle, Screen Test, Sound Stage, Treasure Hunt.

Activities: Box Cars, Chocolate Critters, Comic Strips, Face It!, Face Painting, Finger Funnies, Funny Face, Hairy Head, Hansel And Gretel's House, Photo Paper Dolls, Storybook Theater, Super Stickers.

Food: Colossal Cookie, Painted Cookies, Puffy People, Children's Champagne, Elephant Eggs, Porcupine Pat, Shape Sandwiches, Crazy Cupcakes, Dressy Doll Cake, Dirt and Worms, Ice Cream Clowns.

Favors: Awards and Ribbons, Bug Collection, Bunch of Books, Capes and Hats, Color

Shapes, Comic Books, Puzzlers, Rubber Buggies, Star Cards.

BOUNCY BABY PARTY

It's funny how big kids sometimes like to act like little kids. The Bouncy Baby Party offers a chance for kids of all ages to regress to the bottle and blankie stage. Develop the baby theme by making "diaper" invitations from folded triangles of pink and blue paper secured with diaper pins, to baby bottle favors filled with jelly beans. For a "Come-as-You-Were" invitation, photocopy baby pictures of the special guest of honor, or of the invited guests, and mail them off with the party details.

Invitations: Cookie-on-a-Stick, Cut-Out Kids, Puzzler Invitations, This Is Your Life.

Decorations: All About You, Baby Love, Big & Little, Blast to the Past, Parallel Universe.

Games: Bumbling Bubble Gum, Candy Grab, Candy Wrap, Cocoon, Do-It Dice, Follow the

Footprints, Funny Fashion Show Relay, Giant's Game, Giggle-Gut, Goofy Face, Picture Puzzle, Shoe Loose, Taster's Tongue.

Activities: Box Cars, Face It!, Fashion Fun, Finger Funnies, Funny Face, Gooshy Goo, Photo Paper Dolls, Stork Walkers, Storybook Theater.

Food: Colossal Cookie, Puffy People, Stuffed Bananas, Milk 'n' Cookies Shake, Jell-O Crunch, Dressy Doll Cake, Dirt and Worms.

Favors: Baker's Clay Picture Frames, Me Doll, Thrift Store Ensembles.

CARTOONY PARTY

Sufferin' Succotash! Have a Loony Tunes party complete with all your favorite cartoon or comic characters as guests. Ask the kids to come dressed like the funny pages, then turn them loose in your homemade 'Toon Town. That's all there is to it, folks!

Invitations: Balloon Blimps, Bubble Fun, Color Comics.

Decorations: Billions of Balloons, Candy Land, Comic-Cartoon Town, Disneyroom, Speech Balloons.

Games: Balloon Bodybuilder, Bumbling Bubble Gum, Candy Grab, Cocoon, Follow the Footprints, Funny Fashion Show Relay, Giant's Game, Giggle-Gut, Goofy Face, Picture Puzzle, Screen Test.

Activities: Comic Strips, Face Painting, Fashion Fun, Finger Funnies, Funny Face, Hairy Head, Photo Paper Dolls, Storybook Theater, Super Stickers.

Food: Painted Cookies, Puffy People, Porcupine Pat, Dressy Doll Cake, Surprise-Inside Cake, Dirt and Worms, Ice Cream Clowns.

Favors: Bunch of Books, Coconut Heads, Color Shapes, Comic Books, Face Paints, Magnetic Monsters, Me Doll, Star Cards, Surprise Balls.

CHEERLEADING PARTY

Give me an F! Give me a U! Give me an N! That spells FUN! And so does our Cheerleading Party! Gather a few energetic kids, a handful of pom-poms, and some party spirit! Then let the big game begin! Give me a Y-E-S!

Invitations: Balloon Blimps, Cookie-on-a-Stick, Floral Fantasies, Popper Invitations, Pop-Up Cards, Swirl Stick Invitations.

Decorations: Billions of Balloons, Blast to the Past, Melody Land, Sportsland.

Games: Balloon Bodybuilder, Body Bingo, Bumbling Bubble Gum, Do-It Dice, Funny Fashion Show Relay, Hoppin' Hats, Name the Tune, Oddball Olympics, Pass the Present, Quicksand, Snap—or Zap!, Step 'n' Pop, Tail Tag, Think Fast.

Activities: Bike Bazaar, Bubble Machine, Candy Leis, Fashion Fun, Model Behavior, Popcorn Explosion, Stork Walkers.

Food: Colossal Cookie, Mixin' Munchies, Children's Champagne, Peanut Butter Blitz, Straw Sucker, Brunch-on-a-Stick, Clown Cakes, Dressy Doll Cake, Hamburger Cake, Crispy Crunch Ice Cream Pie.

Favors: Awards and Ribbons, Bubble Stuff, Capes and Hats, Face Paints, Freaky Frisbees,

Me Doll, Pasta Necklaces, Personalized Popcorn Balls, Poppers, Single Cassettes, Surprise Balls, Swirl Sticks, Thrift Store Ensembles, Whistles and Tweeters.

CHEFS IN THE KITCHEN PARTY

Cook up a couple hours of gourmet fun with a Chefs in the Kitchen Party. Have the guests follow the easy recipes in Fun Party Foods to make tempting snacks and goodies. Or let the chefs bake and decorate the birthday cake. Let them find out how much fun making food can be!

Invitations: Bubble Fun, Candy Bars, Cookie-on-a-Stick, Egg-Citing Invitations, Party Menus, Popcorn Party Bags, Recipe Cards.

Decorations: Cafe Partee, Candy Land, Casbah Canopy.

Games: Bumbling Bubble Gum, Candy Grab, Candy Wrap, Mortuary, Poison!, Taster's Tongue.

Activities: Candy Leis, Chocolate Critters, Gooshy Goo, Hansel and Gretel's House, Popcorn Explosion, Salt Scape.

Food: All-You-Can-Eat Buffet, Mixin' Munchies, Painted Cookies, Milk 'n' Cookies Shake, Peanut Butter Blitz, Brunch-on-a-Stick, Jell-O Crunch, Porcupine Pat, Hamburger Cake, Meteor Shower Cake, Surprise-Inside Cake, Chocolate Pasta Ice Cream, Crispy Crunch Ice Cream Pie.

Favors: Baker's Clay Jewelry, Coconut Heads, Edible Jewelry, Meringue Monsters, Pasta Necklaces, Personalized Popcorn Balls, Rabbit-in-a-Hat, Weird Candy.

CHOCOLATE CANDY LAND PARTY

What could be more fun than a party in Chocolate Candy Land? With some mouthwatering imagination, a life-sized Candy Land board game, and lots of melt-in-your-mouth treats, you'll have the sweetest party on the block!

Invitations: Candy Bars, Cookie-on-a-Stick, Egg-Citing Invitations, Popper Invitations, Recipe Cards.

Decorations: Cafe Partee, Candy Land.

Games: Black-Out, Candy Grab, Candy Wrap, Pass the Present, Poison!, Taster's Tongue.

Activities: Candy Leis, Chocolate Critters, Gooshy Goo, Hansel And Gretel's House, Popcorn Explosion, Surprise Bags.

Food: Colossal Cookie, Puffy People, Stuffed Bananas, Chocolate Fizz, Milk 'n' Cookies Shake, Straw Sucker, Jell-O Crunch, Carousel Cake, Crazy Cupcakes, Surprise-Inside Cake, Chocolate Pasta Ice Cream, Crispy Crunch Ice Cream Pie.

Favors: Baker's Clay Jewelry, Coconut Heads, Edible Jewelry, Gold Coins and Funny Money, Meringue Monsters, Pasta Necklaces, Rabbit-in-a-Hat, Secret Stash Trail Mix, Weird Candy.

CLOWN-AROUND PARTY

You never know what kind of fun you'll find under the Big Top. Anything's liable to happen with all those clowns running around. Provide your circus performers with carnival game booths and watch their three-ring circus attractions. Step right up, kids!

Invitations: Balloon Blimps, Bubble Fun, Cookie-on-a-Stick, Floral Fantasies, Magic Wands, Masquerade Disguises, Popcorn Party Bags, Popper Invitations, Pop-Up Cards, Swirl Stick Invitations, Ticket to Fun.

Decorations: Billions of Balloons, Candy Land, Carnival Booths, Casbah Canopy, Disneyroom,

Clowns (see Other Decorating Tips), Melody Land, Tent Safari.

Games: Balloon Bodybuilder, Body Bingo, Boogie Man, Broken Mirror, Bumbling Bubble Gum, Cocoon, Do-It Dice, Funny Fashion Show Relay, Giant's Game, Giggle-Gut, Go Fishing, Goofy Face, Goose Feathers, Hoppin' Hats, Hot Lava, Mind Reader, Oddball Olympics, Quicksand, Screen Test, Tail Tag, Treasure Hunt, Water Balloon Blast-Off, Water Brigade.

Activities: Amazing Swami, Bike Bazaar, Box Cars, Bubble Machine, Candy Leis, Face Painting, Funny Face, Hairy Head, Popcorn Explosion, Pop-Up Clown, Stork Walkers, Surprise Bags.

Food: Colossal Cookie, Mixin' Munchies, Painted Cookies, Children's Champagne, Monkey Milkshake, Straw Sucker, Brunch-on-a-Stick, Elephant Eggs, Carousel Cake, Clown Cakes, Ice Cream Clowns.

Favors: Awards and Ribbons, Bubble Stuff, Capes and Hats, Coconut Heads, Face Paints, Fake Tattoos and Earrings, Magic Cards and Tricks, Makeup Set, Personalized Popcorn Balls, Poppers, Rabbit-in-a-Hat, Surprise Balls, Swirl Sticks, Whistles and Tweeters.

COME-AS-YOU-ARE PARTY

Half the fun of a Come-as-You-Are Party is catching your future guests at odd hours of the day and night. When your unsuspecting friends receive their invitations—by phone or by mail—they're stuck with how they appear at that moment in time for the duration of the party. Watch with surprise, laughs—and sometimes horror—at how they're dressed on arrival.

Invitations: Come-as-You-Are, Cut-Out Kids, Masquerade Disguises, This Is Your Life, Wanted Posters.

Decorations: All About You, Blast to the Past, Cartoon Characters (see Other Decorating Tips), Parallel Universe, Polaroid Pictures or Speech Balloons, Where in the World . . . , Zodiac.

Games: A-B-C Game, Black-Out, Do-It Dice, Follow the Footprints, Funny Fashion Show Relay,

Goofy Face, Heart Surgeon, Mind Reader, Mortuary, Name the Tune, Picture Puzzle, Screen Test, Shoe Loose.

Activities: Amazing Swami, Face It!, Fashion Fun, Funny Face, Model Behavior, Photo Paper Dolls.

Food: Painted Cookies, Puffy People, Porcupine Pat, Dressy Doll Cake, Surprise-Inside Cake.

Favors: Awards and Ribbons, Baker's Clay Picture Frames, Capes and Hats, Coconut Heads, Face Paints, Fake Tattoos and Earrings, False Fingernails, Makeup Set, Me Doll, Personalized Popcorn Balls, Puzzlers, Thrift Store Ensembles.

COOKIE PARTY

You don't have to be a Cookie Monster to enjoy a Cookie Party. You just have to be a cookie lover. Everything—from the invitations to the favors—includes the kids' favorite snack—cookies! Turn on the oven—it's time to bake a Cookie Party!

Invitations: Cookie-on-a-Stick, Party Menus, Recipe Cards.

Decorations: Big & Little cookies (see Other Decorating Tips), Cafe Partee, Candy Land, Hang Up cookies (see Other Decorating Tips).

Games: Candy Grab, Candy Wrap, Pass the Present, Poison!, Taster's Tongue.

Activities: Candy Leis, Hansel And Gretel's House, Surprise Bags.

Food: Colossal Cookie, Painted Cookies, Milk 'n' Cookies Shake, Shape Sandwiches, Blackbeard's Treasure, Crispy Crunch Ice Cream Pie, Dirt and Worms.

Favors: Edible Jewelry, Meringue Monsters, Weird Candy.

CREEPY CRITTER PARTY

A Creepy Critter Party? Sounds crazy, but for some reason the kids love it—and the creepier, the better. Here's a chance for critter lovers to celebrate their crawly friends, right down to a creepy critter cake—a giant caterpillar made from cupcakes lined up and decorated. Our motto? Bugs Are Beautiful!

Invitations: Floral Fantasies, Pogs, Popper Invitations, Pop-Up Cards, Unidentified Flying Objects.

Decorations: Enchanted Forest, Spider's Den, Spooky Cave, Treasure Island, Where in the World . . . .

Games: Boogie Man, Cocoon, Do-It Dice, Follow the Footprints, Giant's Game, Goofy Face, Goose Feathers, Tail Tag, Treasure Hunt.

Activities: Black Hole, Blind Walk, Chocolate Critters, Finger Funnies, Hairy Head.

Food: All-You-Can-Eat Buffet, Mixin' Munchies, Puffy People, Monkey Milkshake, Porcupine Pat, Quicksand Dip, Surprise-Inside Cake, Dirt and Worms, Spider Web Pie.

Favors: Ants-in-the-Sand, Bug Collection, Magnetic Monsters, Meringue Monsters, Rabbit-in-a-Hat, Rubber Buggies.

DAILY PLANET PARTY

Extra! Extra! Calling all reporters! Calling all photographers! Calling all writers and editors and publishers! Paste up a Daily Planet Party featuring headline news from Birthday City, and create your own late-breaking scoop. Ask the guests to come as newspaper staff—reporters or photographers. Have them bring cameras, or you can provide the inexpensive disposable kind. Hand out reporter notebooks to the guests as they walk in the door.

Invitations: Balloon Blimps, Color Comics, Crazy Invitations, Newspaper Headline, Picture Postcards, Swirl Stick Invitations.

Decorations: All About You, Blast to the Past, Comic-Cartoon Town, Polaroid Pictures (see Other Decorating Tips), Where in the World . . . .

Games: A-B-C Game, Bomb Squad, Commercial Crazy, Crime Scene, Detective, Dictionary, Follow the Footprints, Heart Surgeon, Mortuary, Oddball Olympics, Picture Puzzle, Thief!

Activities: Comic Strips, Fashion Fun, Mysterious Message.

Food: Mixin' Munchies, Chocolate Fizz, Bread Bowler, Surprise-Inside Cake, Dirt and Worms.

Favors: Awards and Ribbons, Bunch of Books, Comic Books, Puzzlers, Star Cards.

DANCING WITH A DJ PARTY

Rock the kids to a Dancing with a DJ Party and roll out the good times. Your party will be a hit—as long as the music isn't Mozart. Keep it hip, with hip-hop or rock, and open up the dance floor to the latest moves.

Invitations: Balloon Blimps, Music! Music! Music!, Swirl Stick Invitations, Ticket to Fun.

Decorations: Blast to the Past, Hang Up musical notes (see Other Decorating Tips), Melody Land.

Games: Commercial Crazy, Hot Lava, Name the Tune, Pass the Present, Quicksand, Snap—or Zap!, Sound Stage.

Activities: Model Behavior, Sixties Shirts.

Food: Puffy People, Peanut Butter Blitz, Quicksand Dip, Carousel Cake, Crispy Crunch Ice Cream Pie.

Favors: Single Cassettes, Video Viewing, Whistles and Tweeters.

DOLL AND ACTION FIGURE PARTY

Let the kids invite their special dolls or action figures to the birthday party and have them share the fun with their miniature guests. The entire party can be designed around the big and little couples, from the invitations to the favors.

Invitations: Balloon Blimps, Color Comics, Cut-Out Kids, Masquerade Disguises, Puzzler Invitations, This Is Your Life.

Decorations: All About You, Baby Love, Big & Little (see Other Decorating Tips), Footprints (see Other Decorating Tips), Parallel Universe.

Games: Balloon Bodybuilder, Body Bingo, Bumbling Bubble Gum, Do-It Dice, Follow the Footprints, Funny Fashion Show Relay, Giant's Game, Goofy Face, Heart Surgeon, Mortuary, Oddball Olympics, Picture Puzzle, Shoe Loose, Thief!, Treasure Hunt.

Activities: Box Cars, Comic Strips, Face Painting, Fashion Fun, Hansel And Gretel's House, Model Behavior, Photo Paper Dolls, Pop-Up Clown, Storybook Theater.

Food: All-You-Can-Eat Buffet, Colossal Cookie, Puffy People, Children's Champagne, Elephant Eggs, Shape Sandwiches, Carousel Cake, Dressy Doll Cake, Hamburger Cake, Surprise-Inside Cake, Ice Cream Clowns.

Favors: Baker's Clay Jewelry, Capes and Hats, Coconut Heads, Faux Jewelry, Freaky Frisbees, Me Doll, Personalized Popcorn Balls.

FASHION VICTIM PARTY

First decide whether the party should feature fashion horrors or fashion risks—or both. Any way you design it, it's going to be fashion fun. So dress up, dress down—and put on a fashion showstopper!

Invitations: Come-as-You-Are, Cut-Out Kids, Masquerade Disguises, This Is Your Life.

Decorations: All About You, Blast to the Past, Comic-Cartoon Town, Footprints (see Other Decorating Tips), Parallel Universe, Stars (see Other Decorating Tips), Where in the World . . . .

Games: Balloon Bodybuilder, Body Bingo, Broken Mirror, Cocoon, Follow the Footprints,

Funny Fashion Show Relay, Goofy Face, Hoppin' Hats, Screen Test, Shoe Loose.

Activities: Comic Strips, Face It!, Face Painting, Fashion Fun, Funny Face, Hairy Head, Model Behavior, Photo Paper Dolls, Sixties Shirts, Treasure or Trash?

Food: Banana Butter Buns, Puffy People, Stuffed Bananas, Straw Sucker, Jell-O Crunch, Shape Sandwiches, Crazy Cupcakes, Dressy Doll Cake, Surprise-Inside Cake, Dirt and Worms, Ice Cream Clowns.

Favors: Awards and Ribbons, Baker's Clay Jewelry, Baker's Clay Picture Frames, Capes and Hats, Edible Jewelry, Face Paints, Fake Tattoos and Earrings, False Fingernails, Faux Jewelry, Makeup Set, Me Doll, Pasta Necklaces, Thrift Store Ensembles, White Elephant Gifts.

FREAKY FRIDAY PARTY

Don't freak out! It's just for fun, when the kids come dressed as one another. Instead of having them come to the party as themselves, have them choose a friend—or assign them someone ahead of time—and ask them to dress, talk, and act just like the friend. If you're having boys and girls to the same party, it might be fun to have them come as selected members of the opposite sex.

Invitations: Come-as-You-Are, Cut-Out Kids, Masquerade Disguises, Puzzler Invitations, This Is Your Life.

Decorations: All About You, Parallel Universe, Polaroid Pictures (see Other Decorating Tips), Speech Balloons (see Other Decorating Tips).

Games: Balloon Bodybuilder, Broken Mirror, Funny Fashion Show Relay, Follow the Footprints, Goofy Face, Mind Reader, Picture Puzzle, Screen Test, Shoe Loose.

Activities: Comic Strips, Face It!, Face Painting, Fashion Fun, Funny Face, Hairy Head, Model Behavior, Photo Paper Dolls.

Food: Painted Cookies, Puffy People, Children's Champagne, Shape Sandwiches, Clown Cakes, Surprise-Inside Cake, Dirt and Worms, Ice Cream Clowns.

Favors: Awards and Ribbons, Baker's Clay Picture Frames, Coconut Heads, Face Paints, Makeup Set, Me Doll, Personalized Popcorn Balls, Surprise Balls, Thrift Store Ensembles, White Elephant Gifts.

GAME SHOW PARTY

Hey, birthday kid! Come on down! It's time to play the Game Show Party! Pick out a few favorite game shows you'd like to play with friends, and make those games the focus of your birthday celebration. Spin the Wheel of Fortune, answer the Jeopardy questions, and watch everyone become a winner!

Invitations: Balloon Blimps, Crazy Invitations, Fifty-Two Mix-Up, Funny Money, Masquerade Disguises, Pop-Up Cards, Swirl Stick Invitations, Ticket to Fun.

Decorations: Billions of Balloons, Carnival Booths, Stars, Polaroid Pictures.

Games: A-B-C Game, Black-Out, Body Bingo, Bomb Squad, Bumbling Bubble Gum, Candy Grab, Candy Wrap, Cocoon, Commercial Crazy, Do-It Dice, Giant's Game, Go Fishing, Goose Feathers, Heart Surgeon, Hoppin' Hats, Hot Lava, Name the Tune, Oddball Olympics, Pass the Present, Poison!, Prize Is Right, Quicksand, Snap—or Zap!, Step 'n' Pop, Tail Tag, Think Fast.

Activities: Amazing Swami, Dinosaur Egg Hunt, Pipeline, Stork Walkers, Treasure or Trash?

Food: Colossal Cookie, Children's Champagne, Shape Sandwiches, Blackbeard's Treasure, Surprise-Inside Cake, Crispy Crunch Ice Cream Pie, Igloos.

Favors: Awards and Ribbons, Edible Jewelry, Gold Coins and Funny Money, Magic Cards and Tricks, Pirate Loot, Poppers, Star Cards, Surprise Balls, Video Viewing.

GILLIGAN'S ISLAND PARTY

It was supposed to be a three-hour tour but instead it's a two-hour party, give or take a few minutes! Invite the guests to come as the ship-wrecked characters from the show, then "rescue" them on Gilligan's Island for a tropical birthday party! For a special touch, create a big battered boat from a large cardboard box, shaped and painted to look like the Minnow.

Invitations: Crazy Invitations, Floral Fantasies, Garden Grow, Glow-in-the-Dark Star Chart, Mystery Messages, Newspaper Headline, Pirate's Map, Popper Invitations, Swirl Stick Invitations, Ticket to Fun.

Decorations: Blast to the Past, Enchanted Forest, Hawaiian Island, Parallel Universe, Spider's Den, Spooky Cave, Starry Starry Night, Stars (see Other Decorating Tips), Tent Safari, Treasure Island, Where in the World . . . .

Games: Black-Out, Bomb Squad, Boogie Man, Cocoon, Detective, Do-It Dice, Funny Fashion Show Relay, Giggle-Gut, Go Fishing, Goose Feathers, Hoppin' Hats, Hot Lava, Quicksand, Tail Tag, Treasure Hunt, Water Balloon Blast-Off, Water Brigade.

Activities: Black Hole, Blind Walk, Box Cars, Candy Leis, Creative Construction, Dinosaur Egg Hunt, Galaxy Gazers, Hairy Head, Mysterious Message, Pipeline, Salt Scape, Stork Walkers, Treasure or Trash?

Food: All-You-Can-Eat Buffet, Banana Butter Buns, Mixin' Munchies, Silly Sailboats, Stuffed Bananas, Hawaiian Hurricane, Monkey Milkshake, Bread Bowler, Brunch-on-a-Stick, Elephant Eggs, Porcupine Pat, Quicksand Dip, Blackbeard's Treasure, Meteor Shower Cake, Coffee Can Ice Cream, Dirt and Worms, Igloos, Spider Web Pie.

Favors: Ants-in-the-Sand, Beach Finds, Boats and Floaters, Bug Collection, Coconut Heads, Compass and Treasure Map, Gold Coins and Funny Money, Pirate Loot, Poppers, Rubber Buggies, Secret Stash Trail Mix, Squirt Toys, Thrift Store Ensembles, Water Fun.

GOLD MEDAL GAMES PARTY

Everyone wins a medal—gold, silver, or bronze—at an Olympic Games Party. Invite the amateur athletes, and create your own challenging events or use some of the game suggestions listed below. Let the games begin!

Invitations: Balloon Blimps, Fifty-Two Mix-Up, Picture Postcards, Pogs, Popper Invitations, Swirl Stick Invitations, Ticket to Fun.

Decorations: Billions of Balloons, Carnival Booths, Sportsland, Where in the World . . . .

Games: Balloon Bodybuilder, Body Bingo, Bumbling Bubble Gum, Do-It Dice, Goose Feathers, Hoppin' Hats, Hot Lava, Oddball Olympics, Quicksand, Step 'n' Pop, Tail Tag, Think Fast, Water Balloon Blast-Off, Water Brigade.

Activities: Bike Bazaar, Blind Walk, Creative Construction, Dinosaur Egg Hunt, Pipeline, Stork Walkers.

Food: All-You-Can-Eat Buffet, Colossal Cookie, Potato Puffers, Children's Champagne, Peanut Butter Blitz, Shape Sandwiches, Hamburger Cake, Surprise-Inside Cake, Chocolate Pasta Ice Cream.

Favors: Awards and Ribbons, Capes and Hats, Fake Tattoos and Earrings, Freaky Frisbees, Gold Coins and Funny Money, Pirate Loot, Star Cards, Swirl Sticks, Whistles and Tweeters.

GREAT WHITE SHARK PARTY

"Get out of the water—now!" And head for the Great White Shark Party, where you're the bait! Host your party by the swimming pool, lake, or beach, add a few hungry "sharks"—balloons with shark faces drawn on with permanent felt-tip pen—and watch out! The Great White is looking for you, and you're tasty!

Invitations: Bubble Fun, Picture Postcards, Pirate's Map, Pop-Up Cards.

Decorations: Hawaiian Island or Sunny Day, Treasure Island, Where in the World . . . .

Games: Bomb Squad, Boogie Man, Crime Scene, Detective, Do-It Dice, Go Fishing, Mortuary, Quicksand, Step 'n' Pop, Tail Tag, Think Fast, Water Balloon Blast-Off, Water Brigade.

Activities: Bubble Machine, Pipeline, Salt Scape, Surprise Bags.

Food: Painted Cookies, Puffy People, Hawaiian Hurricane, Peanut Butter Blitz, Quicksand Dip, Shape Sandwiches, Blackbeard's Treasure, Surprise-Inside Cake, Dirt and Worms, Igloos.

Favors: Ants-in-the-Sand, Beach Finds, Boats and Floaters, Bubble Stuff, Compass and Treasure Map, Magnetic Monsters, Pirate Loot, Squirt Toys, Water Fun.

GROW UP! PARTY

Adults are always asking kids, "What do you want to be when you grow up?" Here's a chance for your party guests to make an instant career choice and come dressed as a doctor, lawyer, firefighter, ditch digger, or whatever their favorite occupation might be.

Invitations: Cut-Out Kids, Masquerade Disguises, Newspaper Headline, Puzzler Invitations, This Is Your Life.

Decorations: All About You, Parallel Universe, Polaroid Pictures, Where in the World . . . , Zodiac (see Other Decorating Tips).

Games: Balloon Bodybuilder, Broken Mirror, Funny Fashion Show Relay, Giant's Game, Goofy Face, Heart Surgeon, Mind Reader, Picture Puzzle, Screen Test.

Activities: Comic Strips, Face It!, Face Painting, Hairy Head, Model Behavior, Photo Paper Dolls, Sixties Shirts.

Food: Puffy People, Children's Champagne, Jell-O Crunch, Dressy Doll Cake, Hamburger Cake, Chocolate Pasta Ice Cream, Dirt and Worms.

Favors: Ants-in-the-Sand, Capes and Hats, Coconut Heads, Face Paints, Fake Tattoos and Earrings, False Fingernails, Faux Jewelry, Gold Coins and Funny Money, Makeup Set, Me Doll, Personalized Popcorn Balls, Thrift Store Ensembles.

HAUNTED HOUSE PARTY

Boo! To who? The birthday guest! Here's a scary party that's perfect at Halloween—or anytime the kids want a thrill. Have them come dressed as a favorite evil monster, then create an atmosphere of fear—but not too scary, of course.

Invitations: Crazy Invitations, Glow-in-the-Dark Star Chart, Invisible Invitations, Magic Wands, Masquerade Disguises, Mystery Messages, Puzzler Invitations.

Decorations: Masks, Mystery Mansion, Spider's Den, Spooky Cave.

Games: Black-Out, Bomb Squad, Boogie Man, Cocoon, Crime Scene, Detective, Follow the Footprints, Mortuary, Poison!, Thief!, Treasure Hunt, Winker.

Activities: Amazing Swami, Black Hole, Blind Walk, Ghosts and Goblins, Gooshy Goo, Hairy Head, Mysterious Message, Surprise Bags.

Food: Painted Cookies, Stuffed Bananas, Glow Drink, Bread Bowler, Blackbeard's Treasure, Crazy Cupcakes, Surprise-Inside Cake, Dirt and Worms, Orange Oddballs, Spider Web Pie.

Favors: Ants-in-the-Sand, Bug Collection, False Fingernails, Gold Coins and Funny Money, Magic Cards and Tricks, Pirate Loot, Poppers, Puzzlers, Secret Stash Trail Mix, Surprise Balls, Weird Candy, White Elephant Gifts.

HIPPIE SIXTIES PARTY

Hey, dude! How about a far-out birthday party set in the sixties where all the guests come as hippies? Remember long hair, tie-dyed shirts, psychedelic pants, love-bead necklaces, flower crowns, pink-lens wire glasses, and leather sandals? It's time to groove to the Grateful Dead!

Invitations: Balloon Blimps, Floral Fantasies, Glow-in-the-Dark Star Chart, Music! Music! Music!, Swirl Stick Invitations, This Is Your Life.

Decorations: All About You, Artist Colony, Blast to the Past, Cafe Partee, Melody Land, Stars, Zodiac.

Games: Broken Mirror, Commercial Crazy, Funny Fashion Show Relay, Goofy Face, Name the Tune, Pass the Present, Poison!, Shoe Loose, Sound Stage, Winker.

Activities: Amazing Swami, Bike Bazaar, Blind Walk, Candy Leis, Face Painting, Fashion Fun, Popcorn Explosion, Sixties Shirts, Super Stickers.

Food: All-You-Can-Eat Buffet, Colossal Cookie, Painted Cookies, Straw Sucker, Jell-O Crunch, Crazy Cupcakes, Hamburger Cake, Orange Oddballs.

Favors: Art Box, Baker's Clay Jewelry, Capes and Hats, Edible Jewelry, Face Paints, Faux Jewelry, Magic Cards and Tricks, Pasta Necklaces, Secret Stash Trail Mix, Thrift Store Ensembles.

HOORAY FOR HOLLYWOOD PARTY

Invite the stars to your Hooray For Hollywood Party and watch your celebration sparkle. You never know who might show up: Elvis Presley? Marilyn Monroe? Maybe Frankenstein or even— Barney!

Invitations: Balloon Blimps, Color Comics, Floral Fantasies, Masquerade Disguises, Newspaper Headline, Picture Postcards, Pop-Up Cards, This Is Your Life, Ticket to Fun.

Decorations: Billions of Balloons, Blast to the Past, Cafe Partee, Comic-Cartoon Town, Disneyroom, Melody Land, Polaroid Pictures, Speech Balloons, Starry Starry Night, Stars.

Games: Balloon Bodybuilder, Bomb Squad, Boogie Man, Commercial Crazy, Follow the Footprints, Funny Fashion Show Relay, Goofy Face, Hoppin' Hats, Pass the Present, Picture Puzzle, Prize Is Right, Screen Test, Sound Stage.

Activities: Comic Strips, Face It!, Fashion Fun, Model Behavior, Photo Paper Dolls, Storybook Theater.

Food: Colossal Cookie, Puffy People, Children's Champagne, Shape Sandwiches, Dressy Doll Cake, Spider Web Pie.

Favors: Awards and Ribbons, Baker's Clay Jewelry, Capes and Hats, Edible Jewelry, Face Paints, Fake Tattoos and Earrings, False Fingernails, Faux Jewelry, Gold Coins and Funny Money, Makeup Set, Me Doll, Star Cards, Thrift Store Ensembles, Video Viewing.

HORSIN' AROUND PARTY

Howdy, pardner! How about horsin' around for a little Western-style fun? We'll put on the grub, round up the cowpokes, and head for the celebration corral. Have guests come dressed in Western gear, give them all a bandana to tie around their necks, and decorate the party room with pictures of horses. Now giddy-up! There's a party blowing your way.

Invitations: Picture Postcards, Pop-Up Cards, Puzzler Invitations, Swirl Stick Invitations, Wanted Posters.

Decorations: Carnival Booths, Casbah Canopy, Tent Safari, Treasure Island.

Games: Follow the Footprints, Go Fishing, Goose Feathers, Hoppin' Hats, Oddball Olympics, Step 'n' Pop, Tail Tag, Think Fast.

Activities: Bike Bazaar, Box Cars, Hairy Head, Stork Walkers.

Food: Banana Butter Buns, Mixin' Munchies, Potato Puffers, Chocolate Fizz, Peanut Butter Blitz, Straw Sucker, Bread Bowler, Porcupine Pat, Quicksand Dip, Carousel Cake, Hamburger Cake, Coffee Can Ice Cream, Dirt and Worms, Spider Web Pie.

Favors: Awards and Ribbons, Bunch of Books, Capes and Hats, Secret Stash Trail Mix, Squirt Toys, Thrift Store Ensembles, Whistles and Tweeters.

JURASSIC PARTY

Kids love dinosaurs. The monstrous megasaurs make an ideal theme for a birthday party. So return to the dawn of time and see what kind of prehistoric pets you can conjure up for your Jurassic Party.

Invitations: Egg-Citing Invitations, Pirate's Map, Pop-Up Cards, Unidentified Flying Objects.

Decorations: Big & Little, Blast to the Past, Disneyroom, Enchanted Forest, Spider's Den, Spooky Cave, Tent Safari, Treasure Island, Where in the World . . . .

Games: Bomb Squad, Boogie Man, Cocoon, Giant's Game, Goose Feathers, Hot Lava, Poison!, Quicksand, Sound Stage, Tail Tag, Treasure Hunt.

Activities: Black Hole, Blind Walk, Chocolate Critters, Dinosaur Egg Hunt, Finger Funnies, Ghosts and Goblins, Hairy Head, Pop-Up Clown, Salt Scape, Stork Walkers, Surprise Bags.

Food: Colossal Cookie, Mixin' Munchies, Potato Puffers, Glow Drink, Hawaiian Hurricane, Monkey Milkshake, Bread Bowler, Elephant Eggs, Porcupine Pat, Quicksand Dip, Crazy Cupcakes, Meteor Shower Cake, Surprise-Inside Cake, Dirt

and Worms, Igloos, Orange Oddballs, Spider Web Pie.

Favors: Ants-in-the-Sand, Beach Finds, Bug Collection, Coconut Heads, Compass and Treasure Map, Dinosaur Zoo, Magnetic Monsters, Meringue Monsters, Pirate Loot, Squirt Toys.

MAGICAL PARTY

Abra-ca-dabra! That's all the magic you'll need to create a Magical Party for your child. It's as fun and easy as pulling a rabbit out of a hat. Pull the rest from your imagination, along with a few of the following suggestions.

Invitations: Balloon Blimps, Invisible Invitations, Magic Wands, Mystery Messages, Pop-Up Cards, Puzzler Invitations.

Decorations: Carnival Booths, Casbah Canopy, Mystery Mansion, Spooky Cave.

Games: Bomb Squad, Boogie Man, Broken Mirror, Crime Scene, Detective, Mind Reader, Mortuary, Pass the Present, Picture Puzzle, Poison!, Thief!, Treasure Hunt, Winker.

Activities: Amazing Swami, Black Hole, Blind Walk, Ghosts and Goblins, Mysterious Message, Popcorn Explosion, Surprise Bags.

Food: Painted Cookies, Glow Drink, Quicksand Dip, Surprise-Inside Cake, Dirt and Worms, Igloos.

Favors: Capes and Hats, Magic Cards and Tricks, Secret Stash Trail Mix, Surprise Balls.

MOMMY AND DADDY PARTY

Hey, boys and girls! It's time to grow up—and be just like Mom and Dad. A party offers the perfect opportunity to mimic your parents in dress, word, and deed, and to see what it's like to walk in grown-up shoes for a few hours. Invite the parents to the party, too—dressed as the kids!

Invitations: Balloon Blimps, Cut-Out Kids, Masquerade Disguises, Puzzler Invitations, This Is Your Life.

Decorations: All About You, Baby Love, Blast to the Past, Parallel Universe, Polaroid Pictures.

Games: Balloon Bodybuilder, Black-Out, Body Bingo, Broken Mirror, Commercial Crazy, Do-It Dice, Follow the Footprints, Funny Fashion Show Relay, Giant's Game, Goofy Face, Name the Tune, Picture Puzzle, Screen Test, Shoe Loose.

Activities: Box Cars, Comic Strips, Face It!, Face Painting, Fashion Fun, Funny Face, Hairy Head, Model Behavior, Photo Paper Dolls, Treasure or Trash?

Food: Puffy People, Children's Champagne, Milk 'n' Cookies Shake, Shape Sandwiches, Dressy Doll Cake, Hamburger Cake, Surprise-Inside Cake, Dirt and Worms.

Favors: Capes and Hats, Coconut Heads, Face Paints, Fake Tattoos and Earrings, False Fingernails, Faux Jewelry, Makeup Set, Me Doll, Personalized Popcorn Balls, Puzzlers, Surprise Balls, Thrift Store Ensembles, White Elephant Gifts.

MOTHER GOOSE PARTY

Mary, Mary, quite contrary, how does your party grow? From nursery rhymes and Mother Goose, and then you're set to go! Just pick out your child's favorite rhymes and use them as the theme for your Mother Goose Party. Have the kids come as characters, such as Peter Pumpkin-Eater, Little Bo Peep, or the Dish That Ran Away with the Spoon.

Invitations: Book-a-Party, Color Comics, Cookie-on-a-Stick, Cut-Out Kids, Magic Wands, Pop-Up Cards, Puzzler Invitations.

Decorations: Candy Land, Comic-Cartoon Town, Disneyroom, Enchanted Forest, Treasure Island, Where in the World . . . .

Games: Balloon Bodybuilder, Body Bingo, Boogie Man, Bumbling Bubble Gum, Candy Grab, Follow the Footprints, Funny Fashion Show Relay, Giant's Game, Giggle-Gut, Goofy Face, Name the Tune, Picture Puzzle, Screen Test, Tail Tag.

Activities: Bike Bazaar, Box Cars, Bubble Machine, Chocolate Critters, Comic Strips, Face Painting, Fashion Fun, Hairy Head, Hansel And Gretel's House, Photo Paper Dolls, Pop-Up Clown, Storybook Theater, Super Stickers.

Food: Colossal Cookie, Painted Cookies, Puffy People, Chocolate Fizz, Milk 'n' Cookies Shake, Straw Sucker, Elephant Eggs, Jell-O Crunch, Porcupine Pat, Shape Sandwiches, Blackbeard's Treasure, Carousel Cake, Clown Cakes, Dressy Doll Cake, Dirt and Worms, Ice Cream Clowns, Spider Web Pie.

Favors: Baker's Clay Picture Frames, Bubble Stuff, Bunch of Books, Capes and Hats, Coconut Heads, Color Shapes, Comic Books, Face Paints, Fake Tattoos and Earrings, False Fingernails, Faux Jewelry, Gold Coins and Funny Money, Me Doll, Pirate Loot, Puzzlers, Star Cards, Surprise Balls, Thrift Store Ensembles, Video Viewing.

MOVIE-MAKING PARTY

Lights, camera, action! Anyone can be a star at your Movie-Making Party. With a few costumes, a homemade set, and a fun-to-perform script, you've got the makings of a Birthday Smash Hit! Places everyone . . .

Invitations: Come-as-You-Are, Masquerade Disguises, Picture Postcards, Swirl Stick Invitations, This Is Your Life, Ticket to Fun.

Decorations: All About You, Candy Land, Polaroid Pictures, Stars, Where in the World . . . .

Games: Boogie Man, Commercial Crazy, Follow the Footprints, Funny Fashion Show Relay, Goofy Face, Name the Tune, Picture Puzzle, Screen Test, Sound Stage.

Activities: Amazing Swami, Box Cars, Comic Strips, Face Painting, Fashion Fun, Finger Funnies, Funny Face, Model Behavior, Stork Walkers, Storybook Theater.

Food: Puffy People, Stuffed Bananas, Children's Champagne, Straw Sucker, Brunch-on-a-Stick, Dressy Doll Cake, Chocolate Pasta Ice Cream.

Favors: Awards and Ribbons, Baker's Clay Jewelry, Capes and Hats, Face Paints, Fake Tattoos and Earrings, False Fingernails, Faux Jewelry, Makeup Set, Me Doll, Star Cards, Thrift Store Ensembles, Video Viewing.

MUSICAL PARTY

You don't need musical talent to host a Musical Party. All you need are a few homemade instruments such as coffee can drums, pan lid cymbals, elastic wrist bands with bells, wood blocks, and grain-filled jar shakers; a radio or cassette player; and some helpful suggestions to keep everything in tune. Decorate with cut-out musical notes taped to the walls and hanging from the ceiling, and posters of favorite musical performers.

Invitations: Music! Music! Music!, Swirl Stick Invitations, Ticket to Fun.

Decorations: Melody Land.

Games: Commercial Crazy, Name the Tune, Pass the Present, Screen Test, Snap—or Zap!, Sound Stage.

Activities: Model Behavior, Sixties Shirts.

Food: Painted Cookies, Chocolate Fizz, Straw Sucker, Shape Sandwiches, Carousel Cake, Igloos.

Favors: Awards and Ribbons, Single Cassettes, Video Viewing, Whistles and Tweeters.

MYSTERY MANSION PARTY

With a little detective work, you can turn your party room into a baffling puzzle to solve with a Mystery Mansion Party. Ask the guests to come as a favorite detective, crime solver, police officer, or other related investigating character. Set up a crime scene such as a jewelry store heist, a home burglary, a missing person, or a locked-door puzzle; hand out the magnifying glasses; and go figure!

Invitations: Balloon Blimps, Invisible Invitations, Magic Wands, Mystery Messages, Pirate's Map, Puzzler Invitations.

Decorations: Casbah Canopy, Masks, Mystery Mansion, Spooky Cave, Where in the World . . . .

Games: Black-Out, Bomb Squad, Boogie Man, Cocoon, Crime Scene, Detective, Hot Lava, Mind Reader, Poison!, Quicksand, Thief!, Treasure Hunt.

Activities: Amazing Swami, Black Hole, Blind Walk, Ghosts and Goblins, Mysterious Message, Popcorn Explosion, Surprise Bags.

Food: All-You-Can-Eat Buffet, Glow Drink, Quicksand Dip, Blackbeard's Treasure, Crazy Cupcakes, Surprise-Inside Cake, Dirt and Worms, Spider Web Pie.

Favors: Ants-in-the-Sand, Capes and Hats, Compass and Treasure Map, Magic Cards and Tricks, Pirate Loot, Puzzlers, Rubber Buggies, Secret Stash Trail Mix, Weird Candy, White Elephant Gifts.

PAJAMA PARTY

It doesn't have to be bedtime to host a Pajama Party. Any time of day is fine, as long as all the guests wear their pajamas. Then spend the morning, afternoon, or night playing pajama games!

Invitations: Cut-Out Kids, Glow-in-the-Dark Star Chart, This Is Your Life.

Decorations: All About You, Baby Love, Blast to the Past, Parallel Universe, Starry Starry Night, Tent Safari.

Games: Cocoon, Funny Fashion Show Relay, Giggle-Gut, Screen Test, Shoe Loose, Snap—or Zap!, Winker.

Activities: Amazing Swami, Black Hole, Blind Walk, Face Painting, Fashion Fun, Ghosts and Goblins, Photo Paper Dolls, Popcorn Explosion, Storybook Theater.

Food: All-You-Can-Eat Buffet, Banana Butter Buns, Chocolate Fizz, Glow Drink, Milk 'n' Cookies Shake, Brunch-on-a-Stick, Elephant Eggs, Jell-O Crunch, Dressy Doll Cake, Hamburger Cake, Coffee Can Ice Cream, Igloos.

Favors: Comic Books, Face Paints, Fake Tattoos and Earrings, False Fingernails, Faux Jewelry, Makeup Set, Me Doll, Thrift Store Ensembles, Toothbrush-to-Go.

PET PARTY

Invite your guests—and their pets—to a Pet Party and watch the animal antics begin. You can have the kids bring their stuffed pets or real pets, everything from dogs to cats, mice to rats, hamsters to gerbils, rabbits to turtles. But don't forget the cages and leashes!

Invitations: Cookie-on-a-Stick, Picture Postcards, Pop-Up Cards, Puzzler Invitations.

Decorations: Footprints, Speech Balloons, Spider's Den, Tent Safari.

Games: Cocoon, Do-It Dice, Follow the Footprints, Funny Fashion Show Relay, Go Fishing, Goose Feathers, Tail Tag.

Activities: Chocolate Critters, Dinosaur Egg Hunt, Finger Funnies, Hairy Head, Photo Paper Dolls, Stork Walkers.

Food: Mixin' Munchies, Monkey Milkshake, Elephant Eggs, Porcupine Pat, Surprise-Inside Cake, Dirt and Worms.

Favors: Ants-in-the-Sand, Bug Collection, Coconut Heads, Dinosaur Zoo, Magnetic Monsters, Rabbit-in-a-Hat, Secret Stash Trail Mix, Star Cards.

PHOTO PARTY

Calling all models and photographers. Bring your poses and cameras to a Photo Party and start snapping those pictures. There are lots of way to have fun with a camera, so try some of the suggestions below. Now, watch the birdie and say "Partyyyyy!"

Invitations: Come-as-You-Are, Cut-Out Kids, Masquerade Disguises, Picture Postcards, This Is Your Life, Wanted Posters.

Decorations: All About You, Parallel Universe, Polaroid Pictures, Stars.

Games: Balloon Bodybuilder, Body Bingo, Broken Mirror, Cocoon, Follow the Footprints, Funny Fashion Show Relay, Goofy Face, Oddball Olympics, Picture Puzzle, Screen Test.

Activities: Blind Walk, Box Cars, Face It!, Face Painting, Fashion Fun, Funny Face, Model Behavior, Photo Paper Dolls, Storybook Theater.

Food: Painted Cookies, Children's Champagne, Shape Sandwiches, Dressy Doll Cake, Ice Cream Clowns.

Favors: Art Box, Awards and Ribbons, Baker's Clay Picture Frames, Capes and Hats, Coconut Heads, Face Paints, Makeup Set, Me Doll, Star Cards, Video Viewing.

PIRATE PARTY

Yo-ho! Yo-ho! It's a Pirate's Party for all ye swabs. Ask the guests to dress for the seas, and provide scarves, eye patches, and other accessories to make their costumes come alive. Party on, me hearties, yo-ho!

Invitations: Glow-in-the-Dark Star Chart, Invisible Invitations, Mystery Messages, Pirate's Map, Puzzler Invitations, Swirl Stick Invitations.

Decorations: Casbah Canopy, Disneyroom, Enchanted Forest, Spooky Cave, Starry Starry Night, Tent Safari, Treasure Island.

Games: Bomb Squad, Boogie Man, Candy Grab, Follow the Footprints, Giant's Game, Go Fishing, Heart Surgeon, Hoppin' Hats, Poison!, Quicksand, Step 'n' Pop, Think Fast, Treasure Hunt, Water Balloon Blast-Off, Water Brigade.

Activities: Bike Bazaar, Black Hole, Box Cars, Face It!, Face Painting, Galaxy Gazers, Mysterious Message, Salt Scape, Treasure or Trash?

Food: All-You-Can-Eat Buffet, Potato Puffers, Hawaiian Hurricane, Peanut Butter Blitz, Brunch-on-a-Stick, Quicksand Dip, Blackbeard's Treasure, Dirt and Worms.

Favors: Beach Finds, Capes and Hats, Coconut Heads, Compass and Treasure Map, Face Paints, Fake Tattoos and Earrings, Faux Jewelry, Gold Coins and Funny Money, Pirate Loot, Secret Stash Trail Mix, Squirt Toys, Thrift Store Ensembles, Water Fun, Whistles and Tweeters.

PUNK PARTY

The eighties are over, but they live on at a new-wave Punk Party. When the guests arrive in their torn clothes, offer spray-on temporary hair color in outrageous hues, a few press-on tattoos, and magnetic nose rings to complete the punk look.

Invitations: Crazy Invitations, Cut-Out Kids, Music! Music! Music!, Pogs, This Is Your Life, Ticket to Fun.

Decorations: Artist Colony, Blast to the Past, Cafe Partee, Casbah Canopy, Parallel Universe.

Games: Body Bingo, Boogie Man, Broken Mirror, Funny Fashion Show Relay, Goofy Face, Mortuary, Name the Tune, Shoe Loose, Sound Stage.

Activities: Bike Bazaar, Box Cars, Face It!, Face Painting, Hairy Head, Photo Paper Dolls.

Food: Mixin' Munchies, Straw Sucker, Porcupine Pat, Crazy Cupcakes, Hamburger Cake, Surprise-Inside Cake, Dirt and Worms.

Favors: Ants-in-the-Sand, Art Box, Face Paints, Fake Tattoos and Earrings, False Fingernails, Faux Jewelry, Me Doll, Secret Stash Trail Mix, Single Cassettes, Thrift Store Ensembles, Video Viewing.

PUZZLE PARTY

It's a Puzzle Party and you put it together! Using a variety of puzzling ideas such as jigsaw puzzles, curious questions, treasure hunts, and mysterious messages, create a party that will keep the guests guessing. Make puzzles out of everything from the invitations to the favors.

Invitations: Invisible Invitations, Mystery Messages, Pirate's Map, Puzzler Invitations.

Decorations: Footprints, Mystery Mansion, Parallel Universe, Where in the World . . . .

Games: A-B-C Game, Black-Out, Broken Mirror, Commercial Crazy, Crime Scene, Detective, Mind Reader, Picture Puzzle, Shoe Loose, Treasure Hunt.

Activities: Amazing Swami, Black Hole, Blind Walk, Creative Construction, Mysterious Message, Surprise Bags, Treasure or Trash?

Food: All-You-Can-Eat Buffet, Glow Drink, Jell-O Crunch, Crazy Cupcakes, Surprise-Inside Cake, Dirt and Worms, Orange Oddballs.

Favors: Compass and Treasure Map, Magic Cards and Tricks, Puzzlers, Surprise Balls, White Elephant Gifts.

RESTAURANT PARTY

What's on the menu? A Restaurant Party, right in your own home. With some creative decorating and a few special touches, you can turn the family dining room into a fancy five-star restaurant, a fifties diner, a high-school cafeteria, or a fast-food drive-through.

Invitations: Candy Bars, Cookie-on-a-Stick, Crazy Invitations, Egg-Citing Invitations, Popcorn Party Bags, Popper Invitations, Party Menus, Recipe Cards.

Decorations: Cafe Partee, Candy Land.

Games: A-B-C Game, Black-Out, Bumbling Bubble Gum, Candy Grab, Candy Wrap, Poison!, Taster's Tongue.

Activities: Black Hole, Candy Leis, Dinosaur Egg Hunt, Gooshy Goo, Popcorn Explosion, Salt Scape.

Food: All-You-Can-Eat Buffet, Mixin' Munchies, Painted Cookies, Potato Puffers, Stuffed Bananas, Milk 'n' Cookies Shake, Peanut Butter Blitz, Straw Sucker, Bread Bowler, Brunch-on-a-Stick, Elephant Eggs, Jell-O Crunch, Porcupine Pat, Shape Sandwiches, Hamburger Cake, Chocolate Pasta Ice Cream, Coffee Can Ice Cream.

Favors: Ants-in-the Sand, Baker's Clay Jewelry, Coconut Heads, Edible Jewelry, Gold Coins and Funny Money, Meringue Monsters, Pasta Necklaces, Personalized Popcorn Balls, Rabbit-in-a-Hat, Secret Stash Trail Mix, Weird Candy.

SALON STYLE PARTY

Beauty is only skin deep—but it's fun to get made-up at a Salon Style Party. Give your guests the works—hairstyle, makeup, manicure, and pedicure—just like the salon professionals, at a fraction of the price!

Invitations: Bubble Fun, Cut-Out Kids, Floral Fantasies, Masquerade Disguises, Picture Postcards, This Is Your Life.

Decorations: All About You, Polaroid Pictures, Stars.

Games: Broken Mirror, Commercial Crazy, Funny Fashion Show Relay, Goofy Face, Picture Puzzle, Screen Test, Shoe Loose.

Activities: Candy Leis, Face It!, Face Painting, Fashion Fun, Funny Face, Hairy Head, Model Behavior, Photo Paper Dolls.

Food: Painted Cookies, Puffy People, Children's Champagne, Straw Sucker, Porcupine Pat, Dressy Doll Cake, Crispy Crunch Ice Cream Pie, Igloos, Spider Web Pie.

Favors: Awards and Ribbons, Baker's Clay Jewelry, Baker's Clay Picture Frames, Bubble Stuff, Edible Jewelry, Face Paints, Fake Tattoos and Earrings, False Fingernails, Faux Jewelry, Makeup Set, Me Doll, Star Cards, Thrift Store Ensembles, Video Viewing.

SCARY MONSTER PARTY

Create your own hideous look at a Scary Monster Party, with theatrical makeup, weird wigs, and imagination. Then watch out for Frankenstein, Dracula, the Mummy, or the Blob.

Invitations: Color Comics, Glow-in-the-Dark Star Chart, Invisible Invitations, Masquerade Disguises, Mystery Messages, Pop-Up Cards.

Decorations: Casbah Canopy, Comic-Cartoon Town, Disneyroom, Masks, Mystery Mansion, Spider's Den, Spooky Cave, Where in the World . . . .

Games: Boogie Man, Broken Mirror, Bumbling Bubble Gum, Cocoon, Crime Scene, Detective, Follow the Footprints, Funny Fashion Show Relay, Giant's Game, Goofy Face, Heart Surgeon, Mortuary, Poison!, Quicksand, Thief!

Activities: Black Hole, Blind Walk, Chocolate Critters, Comic Strips, Dinosaur Egg Hunt, Face It!, Face Painting, Fashion Fun, Ghosts and Goblins, Gooshy Goo, Hairy Head, Mysterious Message, Photo Paper Dolls, Surprise Bags.

Food: Colossal Cookie, Painted Cookies, Puffy People, Glow Drink, Monkey Milkshake, Elephant Eggs, Porcupine Pat, Quicksand Dip, Crazy Cupcakes, Surprise-Inside Cake, Dirt and Worms, Spider Web Pie.

Favor: Ants-in-the-Sand, Bug Collection, Dinosaur Zoo, Magnetic Monsters, Meringue Monsters, Pirate Loot, Rubber Buggies, Squirt Toys, Star Cards, Thrift Store Ensembles, Video Viewing, White Elephant Gifts.

SCIENTIFIC EXPEDITION PARTY

Join the famous adventurers who discovered the North Pole, the Mummy's Tomb, the Fountain of Youth, or the Lost Continent. Wearing scientific gear and following a mystifying map, the kids can search for hidden gold, buried treasure, undiscovered artifacts—even unexpected surprises!

Invitations: Egg-Citing Invitations, Floral Fantasies, Glow-in-the-Dark Star Chart, Invisible Invitations, Picture Postcards, Pop-Up Cards, Puzzler Invitations, Ticket to Fun, Unidentified Flying Objects.

Decorations: Blast to the Past, Parallel Universe, Spider's Den, Spooky Cave, Starry Starry Night, Tent Safari, Treasure Island, UFOs (see Other Decorating Tips), Where in the World . . . .

Games: Black-Out, Bomb Squad, Cocoon, Crime Scene, Follow the Footprints, Heart Surgeon, Hot Lava, Mortuary, Poison!, Quicksand, Sound Stage, Taster's Tongue, Thief!, Treasure Hunt.

Activities: Amazing Swami, Bike Bazaar, Black Hole, Blind Walk, Bubble Machine, Dinosaur Egg Hunt, Galaxy Gazers, Gooshy Goo, Hairy Head, Mysterious Message, Pipeline, Popcorn Explosion, Pop-Up Clown, Salt Scape.

Food: All-You-Can-Eat Buffet, Mixin' Munchies, Potato Puffers, Glow Drink, Straw Sucker, Elephant Eggs, Porcupine Pat, Quicksand Dip, Blackbeard's Treasure, Crazy Cupcakes, Meteor Shower Cake, Coffee Can Ice Cream, Dirt and Worms, Igloos, Orange Oddballs, Spider Web Pie.

Favors: Ants-in-the-Sand, Beach Finds, Bubble Stuff, Bug Collection, Compass and Treasure Map, Dinosaur Zoo, Gold Coins and Funny Money, Magnetic Monsters, Pirate Loot, Puzzlers, Rubber Buggies, Secret Stash Trail Mix, Squirt Toys, Swirl Sticks, Water Fun, Weird Candy.

SCI-FI PARTY

Is it real? Or is it fiction? Maybe a little bit of both, when you put on a Sci-Fi Party. Gather guests from outer space, ask them to dress as a favorite sci-fi character, and welcome them to the Planet Birthday, where strange things can happen at any moment. Decorate with moon rocks, stars and planets, posters of Star Trek characters, cardboard cut-outs of space ships, and alien creatures made from construction paper.

Invitations: Color Comics, Glow-in-the-Dark Star Chart, Mystery Messages, Ticket to Fun, Unidentified Flying Objects.

Decorations: Billions of Balloons, Parallel Universe, Starry Starry Night, UFOs, Where in the World . . . .

Games: Cocoon, Funny Fashion Show Relay, Giant's Game, Hot Lava, Quicksand, Treasure Hunt, Water Balloon Blast-Off, Water Brigade.

Activities: Black Hole, Blind Walk, Box Cars, Bubble Machine, Creative Construction, Fashion Fun, Galaxy Gazers, Gooshy Goo, Marble Mania, Mysterious Message, Pipeline, Popcorn Explosion, Salt Scape, Stork Walkers.

Food: Colossal Cookie, Puffy People, Stuffed Bananas, Silly Sailboats, Hawaiian Hurricane, Straw Sucker, Brunch-on-a-Stick, Elephant Eggs, Shape Sandwiches, Meteor Shower Cake, Igloos, Orange Oddballs.

Favors: Ants-in-the-Sand, Bubble Stuff, Freaky Frisbees, Squirt Toys, Surprise Balls, Swirl Sticks, Water Fun, Whistles and Tweeters.

SDRAWKCAB PARTY

Kids love to be silly and there's nothing sillier than doing everything backwards, or inside-out and upside-down. Just keep that in mind while designing your Sdrawkcab Party and everything will turn out simply "lufrednow!" (That's backwards for "wonderful!")

Invitations: Balloon Blimps, Crazy Invitations, Mystery Messages, Pirate's Map, Puzzler Invitations.

Decorations: All About You, Parallel Universe, Polaroid Pictures, Where in the World . . . .

Games: A-B-C Game (Z-X-Y), Broken Mirror, Commercial Crazy, Crime Scene, Do-It (Backwards) Dice, Funny Fashion Show Relay, Oddball Olympics, Treasure Hunt.

Activities: Blind Walk (backwards), Comic Strips, Face Painting, Fashion Fun, Mysterious Message, Treasure or Trash?

Food: All-You-Can-Eat Buffet, Potato Puffers, Straw Sucker, Brunch-on-a-Stick, Shape Sandwiches, Crazy Cupcakes, Hamburger Cake (upside-down), upside-down ice cream sundaes.

Favors: Comic Books, Magic Cards and Tricks, Puzzlers, Surprise Balls.

SECRET SPY PARTY

Calling 007, 008, and all the rest of the double-0 numbers! Let the secret agents go under cover for a Secret Spy Party. A little cloak-and-dagger activity using the games and activities suggested below adds to the suspense. Decorate with secret messages and give everyone a decoder as they enter.

Invitations: Balloon Blimps, Candy Bars, Glow-in-the-Dark Star Chart, Mystery Messages, Popper Invitations, Puzzler Invitations, Unidentified Flying Objects.

Decorations: Casbah Canopy, Mystery Mansion, Parallel Universe, Where in the World . . . .

Games: Bomb Squad, Boogie Man, Broken Mirror, Crime Scene, Hot Lava, Mortuary, Picture Puzzle, Poison!, Quicksand, Thief!, Treasure Hunt.

Activities: Amazing Swami, Blind Walk, Dinosaur Egg Hunt, Face Painting, Fashion Fun, Mysterious Message, Surprise Bags.

Food: Mixin' Munchies, Potato Puffers, Children's Champagne, Glow Drink, Quicksand Dip, Shape Sandwiches, Blackbeard's Treasure, Crazy Cupcakes, Surprise-Inside Cake, Dirt and Worms, Orange Oddballs.

Favors: Capes and Hats, Compass and Treasure Map, Face Paints, Fake Tattoos and Earrings, False Fingernails, Gold Coins and Funny Money, Pirate Loot, Puzzlers, Secret Stash Trail Mix, Squirt Toys, Whistles and Tweeters.

SHERWOOD FOREST PARTY

Bring back the Merry Men of Robin Hood's day with a Sherwood Forest Party. Set the medieval stage, have the guests slip on tights and feather caps, and load up the bows and arrows. It's time to conquer the evil Sheriff of Nottingham!

Invitations: Cookie-on-a-Stick, Glow-in-the-Dark Star Chart, Magic Wands, Masquerade Disguises, Pirate's Map, Swirl Stick Invitations.

Decorations: Blast to the Past, Carnival Booths, Disneyroom, Enchanted Forest, Parallel Universe, Spooky Cave, Starry Starry Night, Tent Safari, Treasure Island, Where in the World . . . .

Games: Balloon Bodybuilder, Body Bingo, Bomb Squad, Boogie Man, Giant's Game, Go Fishing, Goose Feathers, Hoppin' Hats, Hot Lava, Oddball Olympics, Poison!, Quicksand, Step 'n' Pop, Thief!, Treasure Hunt, Water Balloon Blast-Off, Water Brigade.

Activities: Amazing Swami, Bike Bazaar, Black Hole, Blind Walk, Box Cars, Fashion Fun, Pop-Up Clown, Storybook Theater.

Food: Colossal Cookie, Stuffed Bananas, Chocolate Fizz, Bread Bowler, Brunch-on-a-Stick, Blackbeard's Treasure, Carousel Cake, Coffee Can Ice Cream, Dirt and Worms.

Favors: Baker's Clay Jewelry, Capes and Hats, Gold Coins and Funny Money, Squirt Toys, Swirl Sticks, Water Fun.

SKATERS AND BIKERS PARTY

Here's a locomotion party that really moves. Have the kids bring their skates or bikes to the party, design a course to follow, and play follow-the-leader around the park or neighborhood. On your mark, get set, GO!

Invitations: Ticket to Fun, Unidentified Flying Objects.

Decorations: Footprints, Speech Balloons, Where in the World . . . .

Games: Cocoon, Do-It Dice, Follow the Footprints, Hot Lava, Oddball Olympics, Quicksand, Tail Tag, Treasure Hunt.

Activities: Bike Bazaar, Box Cars, Stork Walkers.

Food: Stuffed Bananas, Straw Sucker, Shape Sandwiches, Hamburger Cake, Dirt and Worms.

Favors: Awards and Ribbons, Compass and Treasure Map, Swirl Sticks.

SOCK HOP

We call this a Sock Hop because socks are the article of clothing all guests are required to wear to the party. But you can make it a Hat Hop, a T-Shirt Hop, or base it on other pieces of clothing. Instead of having the kids wear their everyday socks, ask them to come in crazy socks to make it more fun!

Invitations: Cut-Out Kids, Masquerade Disguises, This Is Your Life.

Decorations: All About You, Melody Land.

Games: Broken Mirror, Cocoon, Commercial Crazy, Do-It Dice, Funny Fashion Show Relay, Hoppin' Hats, Name the Tune, Shoe Loose.

Activities: Fashion Fun, Model Behavior, Sixties Shirts.

Food: Mixin' Munchies, Stuffed Bananas, Children's Champagne, Milk 'n' Cookies Shake, Peanut Butter Blitz, Jell-O Crunch, Hamburger Cake, Crispy Crunch Ice Cream Pie.

Favors: Awards and Ribbons, Capes and Hats, Makeup Set, Me Doll, Personalized Popcorn Balls, Single Cassettes, Thrift Store Ensembles.

SOUTH OF THE BORDER PARTY

Set the birthday party in old Mexico for a South of the Border Party. Keep the Hispanic theme in mind while preparing for the amigos, who could wear sombreros, panchos, and sandals.

Invitations: Floral Fantasies, Masquerade Disguises, Picture Postcards, Popper Invitations, Swirl Stick Invitations, Ticket to Fun.

Decorations: Billions of Balloons, Cafe Partee, Carnival Booths, Casbah Canopy, Where in the World . . . .

Games: Commercial Crazy, Go Fishing, Picture Puzzle, Step 'n' Pop, Taster's Tongue.

Activities: Bike Bazaar, Candy Leis, Face Painting.

Food: Colossal Cookie, Mixin' Munchies, Taco Stuffers, Hawaiian Hurricane, Carousel Cake, Clown Cakes, Crispy Crunch Ice Cream Pie.

Favors: Baker's Clay Jewelry, Face Paints, Poppers, Surprise Balls, Swirl Sticks.

SPACE TREK PARTY

Venture where no kid has gone before—into a Space Trek Party! The space cadets should enter your universe dressed as a favorite alien, astronaut, or other space traveler. Start in "Houston"—then lift off for the Final Frontier!

Invitations: Balloon Blimps, Bubble Fun, Glow-in-the-Dark Star Chart, Mystery Messages, Picture Postcards, Ticket to Fun, Unidentified Flying Objects.

Decorations: Billions of Balloons, Parallel Universe, Starry Starry Night, UFOs, Where in the World . . .

Games: Bumbling Bubble Gum, Cocoon, Shoe Loose, Sound Stage, Treasure Hunt.

Activities: Black Hole, Blind Walk, Box Cars, Bubble Machine, Galaxy Gazers, Mysterious Message, Stork Walkers.

Food: Banana Butter Buns, Mixin' Munchies, Glow Drink, Straw Sucker, Bread Bowler, Brunch-on-a-Stick, Crazy Cupcakes, Meteor

Shower Cake, Coffee Can Ice Cream, Orange Oddballs.

Favors: Bubble Stuff, Compass and Treasure Map, Puzzlers, Secret Stash Trail Mix, Star Cards, Swirl Sticks, Weird Candy.

STORYTIME PARTY

A "Once upon a time" party offers a great way to help your child's favorite fictional friends come to life. Invite the guests to dress up as make-believe characters, then wait for Snow White, the Little Mermaid, Mowgli, the Lion King, even Max from *Where the Wild Things Are* to arrive!

Invitations: Book-a-Party, Color Comics, Cut-Out Kids, Picture Postcards, This Is Your Life.

Decorations: Comic-Cartoon Town, Enchanted Forest, Where in the World . . . .

Games: A-B-C Game, Bumbling Bubble Gum, Funny Fashion Show Relay, Giant's Game, Giggle-Gut, Goofy Face, Pass the Present, Picture Puzzle, Snap—or Zap!, Sound Stage.

Activities: Box Cars, Comic Strips, Face It!, Face Painting, Fashion Fun, Finger Funnies, Hairy Head, Hansel and Gretel's House, Photo Paper Dolls, Storybook Theater.

Food: Colossal Cookie, Painted Cookies, Puffy People, Milk 'n' Cookies Shake, Straw Sucker, Porcupine Pat, Shape Sandwiches, Carousel Cake, Clown Cakes, Dressy Doll Cake, Dirt and Worms, Ice Cream Clowns, Spider Web Pie.

Favors: Ants-in-the-Sand, Art Box, Baker's Clay Picture Frames, Bunch of Books, Capes and Hats, Color Shapes, Comic Books, Face Paints, Me Doll, Personalized Popcorn Balls, Star Cards, Surprise Balls, Thrift Store Ensembles, Video Viewing, White Elephant Gifts.

SUMMER IN WINTER PARTY OR WINTER IN SUMMER PARTY

Trapped in the house in the dead of winter? Tired of the relentless sunshine beating down on the hot pavement? Turn that season upside down and host a Summer in Winter or a Winter in Summer Party! All you have to do is pretend it's hot when it's cold—or cold when it's hot!

Invitations: Balloon Blimps, Bubble Fun, Crazy Invitations, Cut-Out Kids, Floral Fantasies, Picture Postcards, Puzzler Invitations.

Decorations: Parallel Universe, Starry Starry Night, Sunny Day, Where in the World . . . .

Games: Broken Mirror, Cocoon, Do-It Dice, Funny Fashion Show Relay, Oddball Olympics, Picture Puzzle, Shoe Loose, Sound Stage, Taster's Tongue, Treasure Hunt.

Activities: Blind Walk, Box Cars, Bubble Machine, Candy Leis, Face It!, Fashion Fun, Photo Paper Dolls, Surprise Bags.

Food: Painted Cookies, Hawaiian Hurricane, Brunch-on-a-Stick, Shape Sandwiches, Surprise-Inside Cake, Dirt and Worms, Igloos.

Favors: Awards and Ribbons, Beach Finds, Bubble Stuff, Capes and Hats, Coconut Heads, Me Doll, Squirt Toys, Surprise Balls, Thrift Store Ensembles, Water Fun, White Elephant Gifts.

SUNRISE SURPRISE PARTY

In this "surprise" party, the birthday person gathers the sleepyhead guests from their nice, warm beds for a birthday party. Just tell the guest's parents your plans ahead of time and ask them to keep it secret!

Invitations: Come-as-You-Are, Mystery Messages, Puzzler Invitations.

Decorations: Billions of Balloons, Cafe Partee, Casbah Canopy, Parallel Universe, Spooky Cave, Starry Starry Night, Tent Safari.

Games: Broken Mirror, Candy Grab, Do-It Dice, Funny Fashion Show Relay, Giggle-Gut, Mind Reader, Poison!, Screen Test, Shoe Loose, Snap—or Zap!, Taster's Tongue, Treasure Hunt.

Activities: Amazing Swami, Candy Leis, Face Painting, Fashion Fun, Model Behavior, Mysterious Message, Photo Paper Dolls, Popcorn Explosion, Surprise Bags, Treasure or Trash?

Food: All-You-Can-Eat Buffet, Banana Butter Buns, Mixin' Munchies, Stuffed Bananas, Silly Sailboats, Children's Champagne, Glow Drink, Brunch-on-a-Stick, Crazy Cupcakes, Dressy Doll Cake, Hamburger Cake, Surprise-Inside Cake, Dirt and Worms, Igloos.

Favors: Awards and Ribbons, Baker's Clay Picture Frames, Capes and Hats, Comic Books, Face Paints, Fake Tattoos and Earrings, False Fingernails, Faux Jewelry, Makeup Set, Me Doll, Pasta Necklaces, Surprise Balls, Thrift Store Ensembles, Toothbrush-to-Go, White Elephant Gifts.

SUPERHEROES PARTY

Is it a bird? Is it a plane? No, it's a Superheroes Party! Look for Superman, Batman, Ninja Turtles, Power Rangers—even Mighty Mouse and Underdog may turn up to save the birthday!

Invitations: Balloon Blimps, Bubble Fun, Color Comics, Cut-Out Kids, Magic Wands, Masquerade Disguises, Mystery Messages, Pogs, Pop-Up Cards, Puzzler Invitations, Swirl Stick Invitations, Unidentified Flying Objects.

Decorations: All About You, Billions of Balloons, Candy Land, Casbah Canopy, Comic-Cartoon Town, Disneyroom, Mystery Mansion, Parallel Universe, Speech Balloons, Spooky Cave, Where in the World . . . .

Games: Balloon Bodybuilder, Body Bingo, Bomb Squad, Boogie Man, Bumbling Bubble Gum, Candy Grab, Cocoon, Crime Scene, Do-It Dice, Funny Fashion Show Relay, Giant's Game, Giggle-Gut, Heart Surgeon, Hot Lava, Mind Reader, Mortuary, Oddball Olympics, Poison!, Quicksand, Treasure Hunt, Water Balloon Blast-Off, Water Brigade.

Activities: Amazing Swami, Bike Bazaar, Black Hole, Blind Walk, Box Cars, Comic Strips, Face It!, Fashion Fun, Ghosts and Goblins, Marble Mania, Mysterious Message, Photo Paper Dolls, Pipeline, Popcorn Explosion, Stork Walkers, Storybook Theater, Super Stickers.

Food: All-You-Can-Eat Buffet, Colossal Cookie, Puffy People, Chocolate Fizz, Peanut Butter Blitz, Elephant Eggs, Quicksand Dip, Hamburger Cake, Meteor Shower Cake, Surprise-Inside Cake, Dirt and Worms, Orange Oddballs, Spider Web Pie.

Favors: Bubble Stuff, Bunch of Books, Capes and Hats, Comic Books, Compass and Treasure Map, Face Paints, Fake Tattoos and Earrings, Me Doll, Puzzlers, Secret Stash Trail Mix, Squirt Toys, Swirl Sticks, Thrift Store Ensembles, Whistles and Tweeters.

TALENT SHOW PARTY

Hey kids! Why don't we put on a show? No need for tryouts—everybody at the Talent Show Party has got a song, dance, or comedy routine to share. Be sure to record it on videotape to play back to the party audience!

Invitations: Music! Music! Music!, Pop-Up Cards, Swirl Stick Invitations, This Is Your Life, Ticket to Fun.

Decorations: All About You, Billions of Balloons, Casbah Canopy, Melody Land, Polaroid Pictures, Stars.

Games: Commercial Crazy, Do-It Dice, Funny Fashion Show Relay, Oddball Olympics, Screen Test, Sound Stage.

Activities: Amazing Swami, Fashion Fun, Model Behavior, Storybook Theater.

Food: Colossal Cookie, Painted Cookies, Puffy People, Straw Sucker, Jell-O Crunch, Dressy Doll Cake, Surprise-Inside Cake, Crispy Crunch Ice Cream Pie.

Favors: Awards and Ribbons, Capes and Hats, Face Paints, Makeup Set, Single Cassettes, Star Cards, Thrift Store Ensembles, Video Viewing.

TEDDY BEAR PICNIC

Invite the kids and their special guests to your Teddy Bear Picnic to celebrate your child's "bearthday." Each guest brings a favorite stuffed animal—preferably a bear, but any kind will do—then share the fun with the bears!

Invitations: Cookie-on-a-Stick, Cut-Out Kids, Picture Postcards, Pop-Up Cards.

Decorations: Carnival Booths, Enchanted Forest, Spooky Cave, Tent Safari.

Games: Boogie Man, Cocoon, Giant's Game, Oddball Olympics, Picture Puzzle, Tail Tag, Treasure Hunt.

Activities: Black Hole, Blind Walk, Chocolate Critters, Face It!, Finger Funnies, Hairy Head, Stork Walkers, Storybook Theater.

Food: Banana Butter Buns, Colossal Cookie, Stuffed Bananas, Chocolate Fizz, Elephant Eggs, Porcupine Pat, Shape Sandwiches, Crazy Cupcakes, Surprise-Inside Cake, Dirt and Worms.

Favors: Ants-in-the-Sand, Bug Collection, Coconut Heads, Magnetic Monsters, Rabbit-in-a-Hat, Secret Stash Trail Mix.

THIS IS YOUR LIFE PARTY

Hey, birthday kid! This is your life! And what a life it's been so far, as you'll see when all the special surprise guests suddenly appear to remind you of your childhood! (Was it only yesterday . . . ?)

Invitations: Come-as-You-Are, Cut-Out Kids, Masquerade Disguises, Newspaper Headline, Swirl Stick Invitations, This Is Your Life, Wanted Posters.

Decorations: All About You, Baby Love, Blast to the Past, Parallel Universe, Where in the World . . . .

Games: A-B-C Game, Black-Out, Broken Mirror, Cocoon, Do-It Dice, Funny Fashion Show Relay, Mind Reader, Picture Puzzle, Screen Test, Shoe Loose, Sound Stage, Treasure Hunt.

Activities: Amazing Swami, Black Hole, Blind Walk, Face It!, Fashion Fun, Photo Paper Dolls, Surprise Bags, Treasure or Trash?

Food: Colossal Cookie, Painted Cookies, Puffy People, Children's Champagne, Shape Sandwiches, Dressy Doll Cake, Surprise-Inside Cake, Ice Cream Clowns.

Favors: Baker's Clay Picture Frames, Coconut Heads, Me Doll, Personalized Popcorn Balls, Single Cassettes, Star Cards, Surprise Balls, Video Viewing, White Elephant Gifts.

TRAINS, PLANES, AND AUTOMOBILES PARTY

A transportation party? Sure! Kids are fascinated with trains, planes, boats, and cars, so why not feature one or all at the birthday party. Create some ways to travel down the highway of fun—or use some of the following ideas.

Invitations: Balloon Blimps, Bubble Fun, Pirate's Map, Puzzler Invitations, Swirl Sticks, Ticket to Fun, Unidentified Flying Objects.

Decorations: Billions of Balloons, Candy Land, Disneyroom, Enchanted Forest, Hawaiian Island, Parallel Universe, Tent Safari, Where in the World . . . .

Games: A-B-C Game, Bomb Squad, Broken Mirror, Funny Fashion Show Relay, Hot Lava, Pass the Present, Picture Puzzle, Quicksand, Snap— or Zap!, Treasure Hunt.

Activities: Bike Bazaar, Blind Walk, Box Cars, Pipeline, Stork Walkers.

Food: All-You-Can-Eat Buffet, Hawaiian Hurricane, Shape Sandwiches, Carousel Cake, Surprise-Inside Cake, Igloos.

Favors: Ants-in-the-Sand, Beach Finds, Boats and Floaters, Compass and Treasure Map, Surprise Balls, Water Fun.

TROPICAL LUAU

Set your birthday party in the Pacific Islands with a Tropical Luau. Let the kids come in grass skirts, bathing suits, colorful Hawaiian shirts or jams, then treat them to a few hours in a Polynesian paradise.

Invitations: Bubble Fun, Floral Fantasies, Picture Postcards, Pirate's Map, Pop-Up Cards, Swirl Stick Invitations, Ticket to Fun.

Decorations: Billions of Balloons, Carnival Booths, Casbah Canopy, Disneyroom, Hawaiian

Island (see Other Decorating Tips), Starry Starry Night, Tent Safari, Treasure Island, Where in the World . . . .

Games: Candy Grab, Cocoon, Funny Fashion Show Relay, Go Fishing, Goose Feathers, Hot Lava, Quicksand, Tail Tag, Treasure Hunt, Water Balloon Blast-Off, Water Brigade.

Activities: Amazing Swami, Blind Walk, Bubble Machine, Candy Leis, Dinosaur Egg Hunt, Face Painting, Fashion Fun, Hairy Head, Salt Scape, Stork Walkers.

Food: Banana Butter Buns, Painted Cookies, Stuffed Bananas, Silly Sailboats, Hawaiian Hurricane, Monkey Milkshake, Straw Sucker, Brunch-on-a-Stick, Porcupine Pat, Quicksand Dip, Blackbeard's Treasure, Carousel Cake, Meteor Shower Cake, Dirt and Worms, Igloos.

Favors: Ants-in-the-Sand, Beach Finds, Boats and Floaters, Bubble Stuff, Coconut Heads, Compass and Treasure Map, Face Paints, Freaky Frisbees, Pasta Necklaces, Poppers, Squirt Toys, Swirl Sticks, Water Fun.

UNDER THE SEA PARTY

With a little effort, you can turn the party room into an ocean for an Under the Sea Party! Cover the walls with blue tissue paper, add pictures of colorful tropical fish cut out of magazines or create some out of construction paper, dim the lights, turn on the music from *The Little Mermaid,* and get into bathing suits. When everything is ready, welcome the mermaids, sharks, catfish, starfish, and the rest of the marine world gang.

Invitations: Bubble Fun, Cookie-on-a-Stick, Floral Fantasies, Picture Postcards, Pirate's Map, Ticket to Fun.

Decorations: Billions of Balloons, Spooky Cave, Treasure Island, Where in the World . . . .

Games: Bumbling Bubble Gum, Cocoon, Do-It Dice, Go Fishing, Hot Lava, Oddball Olympics, Quicksand, Tail Tag, Treasure Hunt, Water Balloon Blast-Off, Water Brigade.

Activities: Black Hole, Blind Walk, Bubble Machine, Pipeline, Salt Scape.

Food: Mixin' Munchies, Stuffed Bananas, Silly Sailboats, Hawaiian Hurricane, Monkey Milkshake, Straw Sucker, Quicksand Dip, Blackbeard's Treasure, Meteor Shower Cake, Surprise-Inside Cake, Dirt and Worms, Igloos, Orange Oddballs.

Favors: Ants-in-the-Sand, Beach Finds, Boats and Floaters, Bubble Stuff, Coconut Heads, Compass and Treasure Map, Pirate Loot, Squirt Toys, Water Fun.

VIDEO GAME PARTY

It's a Video Game Party, with round-robin challengers, play-offs, and winners! Ask your guests to bring their favorite video games to share, then prepare for the fast-action tournament.

Invitations: Music! Music! Music!, Pogs, Pop-Up Cards, Ticket to Fun.

Decorations: Carnival Booths, Disneyroom.

Games: Commercial Crazy, Picture Puzzle, Sound Stage.

Activities: Photo Paper Dolls, Pipeline, Popcorn Explosion, Super Stickers.

Food: Painted Cookies, Milk 'n' Cookies Shake, Shape Sandwiches, Hamburger Cake, Surprise-Inside Cake, Dirt and Worms, Ice Cream Clowns.

Favors: Awards and Ribbons, Color Shapes, Puzzlers, Star Cards, Video Viewing.

WATER WORLD PARTY

Here's a simple recipe to guarantee party fun—just add water! A hot summer day is the perfect time for a Water World Party—at the kiddy pool, in the sprinkler, or at the beach.

Invitations: Balloon Blimps, Bubble Fun, Pirate's Map.

Decorations: Treasure Island, Where in the World . . . .

Games: Balloon Bodybuilder, Body Bingo, Do-It Dice, Funny Fashion Show Relay, Go Fishing, Goose Feathers, Hot Lava, Oddball Olympics, Quicksand, Treasure Hunt, Water Balloon Blast-Off, Water Brigade.

Activities: Blind Walk, Bubble Machine, Pipeline, Salt Scape.

Food: Banana Butter Buns, Silly Sailboats, Chocolate Fizz, Hawaiian Hurricane, Straw Sucker, Porcupine Pat, Quicksand Dip, Blackbeard's Treasure, Surprise-Inside Cake, Coffee Can Ice Cream, Dirt and Worms, Igloos, Orange Oddballs.

Favors: Ants-in-the-Sand, Beach Finds, Boats and Floaters, Bubble Stuff, Pirate Loot, Squirt Toys, Water Fun.

WHERE IN THE WORLD . . . PARTY

Around the world in about two hours? They said it couldn't be done. Set up exotic locations in your home and you can take the kids on a tour of the planet by visiting Alaska, Africa, France, Italy, Russia, South America, China, and Japan and have them back in time for cake and ice cream! Tickets, please. All aboard!

Invitations: Mystery Messages, Picture Postcards, Pirate's Map, Puzzler Invitations, Ticket to Fun, Unidentified Flying Objects.

Decorations: Candy Land, Disneyroom, Parallel Universe, Test Safari, Treasure Island, Where in the World . . . .

Games: A-B-C Game, Broken Mirror, Commercial Crazy, Funny Fashion Show Relay, Hoppin'

Hats, Name the Tune, Pass the Present, Picture Puzzle, Poison!, Quicksand, Shoe Loose, Taster's Tongue, Treasure Hunt.

Activities: Amazing Swami, Bike Bazaar, Blind Walk, Box Cars, Dinosaur Egg Hunt, Face It!, Fashion Fun, Galaxy Gazers, Photo Paper Dolls, Salt Scape, Stork Walkers, Treasure or Trash?

Food: All-You-Can-Eat Buffet, Mixin' Munchies, Peanut Butter Blitz, Brunch-on-a-Stick, Shape Sandwiches, Meteor Shower Cake, Surprise-Inside Cake, Dirt and Worms, Igloos, Orange Oddballs.

Favors: Baker's Clay Picture Frames, Beach Finds, Bunch of Books, Capes and Hats, Coconut Heads, Comic Books, Compass and Treasure Map, Gold Coins and Funny Money, White Elephant Gifts.

ZOO PARTY

Lions and tigers and bears? Oh my! And that's not all you may see at a Zoo Party. Take the kids to an actual zoo for fun—or have the zoo right at home, where the guests come as wild animals while you provide the cardboard-box cages and zoo food.

Invitations: Cookie-on-a-Stick, Picture Postcards, Pop-Up Cards, Puzzler Invitations, Ticket to Fun.

Decorations: Carnival Booths, Disneyroom, Enchanted Forest, Spider's Den, Spooky Cave, Tent Safari, Treasure Island, Where in the World . . . .

Games: A-B-C Game, Bumbling Bubble Gum, Candy Grab, Cocoon, Do-It Dice, Funny Fashion Show Relay, Giant's Game, Go Fishing, Goose Feathers, Picture Puzzle, Tail Tag.

Activities: Blind Walk, Box Cars, Chocolate Critters, Dinosaur Egg Hunt, Face It!, Finger Funnies, Hairy Head, Photo Paper Dolls, Popcorn Explosion, Stork Walkers.

Food: Banana Butter Buns, Mixin' Munchies, Potato Puffers, Stuffed Bananas, Monkey Milkshake, Straw Sucker, Elephant Eggs, Porcupine

Pat, Sandwich Shapes, Carousel Cake, Clown Cakes, Hamburger Cake, Surprise-Inside Cake, Dirt and Worms, Ice Cream Clowns.

Favors: Ants-in-the-Sand, Bug Collection, Coconut Heads, Dinosaur Zoo, Magnetic Monsters, Meringue Monsters, Rabbit-in-a-Hat, Rubber Buggies, Secret Stash Trail Mix, Star Cards, White Elephant Gifts.

INVENTIVE
INVITATIONS

Set the stage for the special occasion with creative and personalized invitations to the selected guests. Keep it simple and use basic arts and crafts materials, such as construction paper, fancy stationery, picture postcards, or colorful tagboard. Write the party details on each invitation using felt-tip pens, scented pens, write-over markers, puffy paints, poster paints, watercolors, or crayons. Decorate with stickers, glitter, sequins, magazine cut-outs, photographs, yarn, ribbon, or whatever else might add some pizzazz.

Or use one of the ideas in this chapter to welcome the guests to the birthday celebration in a unique and festive way. There are lots of suggestions to choose from, so select the one that best matches your party theme.

When the invitations are ready to go, mail them in fancy envelopes, large mailers, small boxes, or paper tubes. Hand deliver the invitations if they're delicate, awkward, or breakable—and the guests live nearby. Depending on the type of party you're hosting, you might simply make a phone call to the guests and their parents to explain the party details.

If you're mailing the invitations, send them out a week or two before the party date, to be sure they arrive on time. The following basic party details should be included on each invitation:

* The birthday child's name
* The host's name
* The address of the party
* A map showing how to get there
* The date of the party
* The starting *and* ending times
* The RSVP date
* The host's telephone number

You might also want to include the following:

* The type of food you'll be serving, especially if the party occurs near breakfast, lunch, or dinner time
* Any special items required, such as a bicycle, odd gift, or sleeping bag
* What to wear, such as a costume, bathing suit, or pajamas

And if it's a surprise party, write "SHHHH! IT'S A SURPRISE!" or "KEEP IT A SECRET!" in big capital letters so no one ruins the surprise.

Here are some invitation ideas to help you welcome your guests to the party!

BALLOON BLIMPS

There's a surprise in the mailbox when your guests receive this Balloon Blimp—especially when it turns out to be a party invitation! Just tell your friends to blow up the balloon and discover the party details.

MATERIALS

* Large round balloon, deflated, for each guest
* Colorful permanent felt-tip pens
* Confetti, glitter, or colored rice
* Funnel

WHAT TO DO

Inflate a balloon but do not tie it off. With assistance from another pair of hands to hold the end of the balloon closed, write the party details on the balloon's surface using a permanent felt-tip pen. Decorate with a funny face or designs, if you like. Let the air out, then insert the end of the funnel into the balloon opening and pour in some confetti, glitter, or colored rice. Place the balloon in an envelope with a note instructing the guests to blow up the Balloon Blimp. Repeat the process with the other balloons. Mail to guests.

BOOK-A-PARTY

Choose a favorite children's book and use it as a guide for creating "literary" invitations for your guests.

MATERIALS

* Inexpensive children's books
* White construction paper
* Black felt-tip pens
* Glue, tape, scissors

WHAT TO DO

Buy several inexpensive children's books that your child likes or that feature a birthday party as the theme. Make photocopies of a photograph of your child and replace the featured character in the book with your child's picture. Draw and cut out speech balloons out of the white construction paper. Write the party details on the balloons and glue them into place. Mail the whole books in padded envelopes, or tear pages from the books to mail individually to guests.

BUBBLE FUN

Kids love bubbles—and that's why using one of the following ideas is a great way to invite guests to a birthday party!

MATERIALS

* Package of bubble bath for each guest
* Bottle of bubble solution for each guest
* Pink construction paper
* Bubble gum
* Black felt-tip pen
* Tape, scissors

WHAT TO DO

Write the party details on the outside of the bubble bath packages in black felt-tip pen. Place in envelopes and mail to guests.

Or write the party details on the bubble solution bottles. Hand deliver to friends by blowing some bubbles outside the front door, ringing the doorbell, leaving the bubble solution on the doorstep, and disappearing.

Or cut large bubble shapes out of pink construction paper and write the party details on them with black felt-tip pen. Tape on a pack of bubble gum to each bubble. Place in envelopes and mail to guests.

CANDY BARS

Imagine receiving a candy bar in the mail! Imagine opening up the candy bar and finding a birthday party invitation inside! It doesn't get better than this.

MATERIALS

* Rectangular candy bar wrapped in paper for each guest
* White paper
* Felt-tip pens
* Scissors, tape

WHAT TO DO

Open the candy bars carefully, trying not to tear the wrapper. Write party details on pieces of the white paper cut to the size of the candy bar. Place the invitations inside the wraps and reseal the candy bars with tape. Wrap each candy bar in gift wrap and mail in a padded envelope or small box, or hand deliver to friends.

COLOR COMICS

Open the Sunday funny pages and have Calvin and Hobbes, Garfield, or Cathy invite the guests to your birthday party with colorful, comical invitations.

MATERIALS

* Color comic pages
* Glue, scissors
* White correction fluid
* Tagboard
* Fine point felt-tip pen

WHAT TO DO

Find your favorite comics in the Sunday papers or in comic books, and cut out strips to send to each guest. Glue the comic strips onto tagboard strips cut to size. Using white correction fluid, carefully cover over the writing in the speech balloons and allow to dry. Fill in blank speech balloons with funny sayings personalized for each guest, then write the party details in the last bubble. Place in envelopes large enough to hold a comic strip, then decorate envelopes with cut-out comics. Draw speech balloons around the guest's address and the return address on each envelope.

COME-AS-YOU-ARE

Your guests will never know exactly when the invitation will arrive with a Come-as-You-Are party. Half the fun is catching the kids in the middle of whatever they're doing—and making sure they look the same way when they come to the party.

MATERIALS

* Telephone
* Guest list with phone numbers

WHAT TO DO

Make up the guest list complete with telephone numbers, then plan different times of the day to call your friends. You might want to call early in the morning to catch them with "pillow hair," late at night to catch them in pajamas, in the middle of lunch to catch them eating a sandwich, in the car (if they have a car phone), after school when they're tired and sweaty, or before church when they're all dressed up—any time of day or night! When you call, ask your guests what they are doing and what they are wearing. Then tell them they are to come to the party dressed exactly that way—in pajamas or in a bathing suit, for example. If you prefer, mail the invitations instead of calling, and ask your guests to come as they are at a specified time and place, such as dinner time, girl/boy scout meeting time, bath time, bedtime, or whatever time you decide.

COOKIE-ON-A-STICK

Here's a tasty invitation the guests can eat after they read the party details. Be sure to hand deliver these Cookie-on-a-Stick invitations so they don't end up as cookie crumbs instead. Use our cookie recipe below, or your favorite sugar or gingerbread cookie recipe.

MATERIALS

* 4 cups flour
* 1/2 cup honey
* 1 cup margarine
* 1 beaten egg
* Large, star-shaped cookie cutter or other cookie shape
* Wooden ice cream sticks
* Tubes of colored frosting with tips
* Felt-tip pens

WHAT TO DO

Mix flour, honey, margarine, and egg together and chill dough 2 hours, or until firm. Preheat the oven to 350 degrees. Roll dough to 1/2 inch thick and cut into stars or other shapes. Place on a well-greased cookie sheet and bake 6 to 8 minutes. Insert ice cream sticks into cookies while still warm. When cookies are cool and

firm, decorate as desired, and write the party details on them with the frosting. Or write each guest's name in the center of the cookie with the frosting, and write the party details on the stick using a felt-tip pen. Handle cookie invitations carefully and hand deliver to guests.

CRAZY INVITATIONS

Just about anything will work as a fun invitation to your party. Use your imagination and you'll be surprised what you come up with. Here are some unusual suggestions for crazy invitations. Keep your theme in mind as you select the most appropriate invitation for your party.

MATERIALS

* Apron
* Baby Bottle
* Book
* Candy Bar
* Cereal Box
* Coconut
* Comic Book
* Art
* Ball
* Calendar
* Carry Bag
* Clam Shell
* Comb and Brush
* Computer Disk

* Cookies
* Deck of Cards
* Egg
* Flashlight
* Garden Glove
* Harmonica
* Instrument
* Life Savers
* Magazine

* Music Sheet
* Notebook
* Pencil
* Ribbon
* Scarf
* Snack
* Squirt Gun
* Sunglasses
* Toothbrush
* Underwear
* Water Bottle

* Curlers
* Doll
* Felt-Tip Pen
* Frisbee
* Gum
* Hat
* Jack O'Lantern
* Light Bulb
* Microwave Popcorn Bag
* Night Light
* Origami Paper
* Poster
* Rubber Spider
* Seed Packet
* Sock
* Stuffed Animal
* T-Shirt
* Towel
* Valentine
* Yo-Yo

* Permanent felt-tip pen
* Blank white cards
* String, ribbon, tape

WHAT TO DO

Select a crazy invitation item and buy one for each guest, or get a variety of items and send a different one to each guest. If possible, write your party details directly on the items with permanent felt-tip pen. If not, write the details on a small card and attach it to the item with string, ribbon, or tape. Hand deliver the invitations, or leave them on the doorstep, ring the bell, and disappear. You might also have a messenger deliver the invitations, or mail them either in padded envelopes or wrapped in tissue paper inside small boxes.

CUT-OUT KIDS

The guests can play with these Cut-Out Kid invitations after they've read the party details. To make it more fun, use cut-out pictures of each friend's face to place on their own paper doll's head.

MATERIALS

* Heavy white tagboard or store-bought paper dolls
* Magazines
* White paper
* Colorful felt-tip pens
* Scissors, glue
* Pictures of the party guests, if possible

WHAT TO DO

Use a paper doll as a pattern to create your Cut-Out Kid invitations, or draw your own on heavy white tagboard. (If you prefer, use store-bought paper dolls.) Cut out the paper dolls and either glue on the faces of your party guests, or draw on faces to look like the guests. Write the party details on the back of each paper doll. Cut out clothes from magazines that fit the doll, or create your own out of the white paper. Glue on the clothes to the dolls. Mail the invitations to your guests. You might want to ask them to bring their paper dolls to the party, each with an outfit they have designed and created. And invite the guests'

favorite dolls to the party, too, if you like. Don't limit this idea to dolls—you also can use animal or monster cut-outs.

EGG-CITING INVITATIONS

There are lots of ways to invite your guests to your birthday party using a variety of egg-stra-ordinary ideas.

MATERIALS

* White tagboard
* Picture of birthday child
* Scissors, glue
* Plastic egg or real egg for each guest
* Fillers, such as tiny toys, candies, or confetti
* White adhesive tape
* Permanent felt-tip pens

WHAT TO DO

You can make simple egg invitations by cutting white tagboard into oval shapes and writing the party details on one side. On the other side, glue on a picture of a birthday cake, the party guest of honor, or a small animal, then mail to guests.

Or buy some small plastic eggs at the hobby or toy store. Open them up and fill them with small toys, candies, or confetti, along with a folded note describing the party details. Place in small boxes and mail to guests. Or hollow out real eggs by poking a small hole in one end of the egg and pouring out the contents. Rinse the eggs and let them dry, then fill them with confetti. Cover the hole on each egg with white adhesive tape. Write the party details around the outside of each egg and place in small padded boxes. Mail to guests. Ask them to bring the filled eggs to the party to break over one another's heads!

FIFTY-TWO MIX-UP

Drive your guests crazy with a birthday party card game that takes them time to assemble!

MATERIALS

* An inexpensive deck of cards for each guest
* Permanent felt-tip pens

WHAT TO DO

Write your party invitation on a separate sheet of paper to use as a guide. Try to make it exactly fifty-two words long. Using one deck of cards per invitation, write one word of the invitation on its own card. Shuffle the deck, replace the cards into the pack. Repeat for all guests. Mail the decks in small padded envelopes, telling the guests they must put the cards together in the proper order to read the special message.

FLORAL FANTASIES

Create colorful and festive Floral Fantasies the kids can keep as decorations for their rooms. This also makes a great activity at the party.

MATERIALS

* 8 sheets tissue paper per guest, any size, in a variety of colors
* 1 foot of string per flower
* 1 foot of bendable floral wire per flower
* Colorful felt-tip pens

WHAT TO DO

For each floral fantasy, separate the colored tissue sheets and layer in piles of eight using a variety of colors. Beginning at the shorter end of the tissue paper rectangle, fold the tissue accordion-style. Use the string to tie the tissue paper in the middle. Peel back half the layers to one side, then the other. Turn the flower upside down and repeat, peeling back layers until the flower is fluffy and full. Wrap bendable wire around the center, and twist together the ends to form a stem. Write party details with felt-tip pen inside the layers of the flower or attach a separate card to the flower and place in a box for mailing, or hand deliver to guests.

FUNNY MONEY

You don't have to pay your guests to come to your party, but you could invite them with some funny money.

MATERIALS

* Play paper money, play coins, chocolate coins in gold foil
* White correction fluid
* Picture of birthday child
* Felt-tip pens, scissors

WHAT TO DO

Buy play money to send to each guest. Cover some of the writing with correction fluid, allow to dry, and fill in with the party details. Or photocopy a dollar bill, substituting your child's picture for the president. Cover some areas of the photocopied dollar with correction fluid, allow to dry, and replace with party details. Include some chocolate coins with the envelope and mail to guests. Tell the guests to bring the funny money to the party to exchange for "valuable prizes" while playing the Prize Is Right or to buy White Elephant Gifts.

GARDEN GROW

Give your guests the gift of life that doubles as a party invitation, so they can watch the fun grow.

MATERIALS

* Seed packets or beans
* Small plastic plant containers
* Potting soil
* Permanent felt-tip pens

WHAT TO DO

The easy way to invite your guests to a garden party, jungle adventure, or other plant-themed party is to write the party invitations on the outside of flower seed packets and mail them in an envelope decorated with flower stickers.

It's even more fun to use your green thumb and plant the invitations to your guests. Fill the small plastic plant containers with potting soil. Sow in flower or vegetables seeds, or plant beans or grass, which grow quickly. Write the party details on the planter with felt-tip pens, as well as instructions on how to care for the plants. When the party day arrives, the seeds should have sprouted, so the guests can bring their seedlings along. Award a prize for the biggest, the littlest, the cutest, and the greenest plant.

GLOW-IN-THE-DARK STAR CHART

A unique invitation that can only be viewed at night. Watch it come to life when the lights go out!

MATERIALS

* Glow-in-the-dark paint or pens (available at hobby and toy stores)
* A chart of the stars and planets

* White tagboard
* Glue

WHAT TO DO

Find a chart of the stars in a library book and make a photocopy for each guest. Glue the chart on to white tagboard. Paint or draw over each star with glow-in-the-dark paint. Paint or draw the party details around the edges or on the back of the tagboard using the glow-in-the-dark paint or pens. Place the charts in large envelopes and glue star stickers to the outside—glow-in-the-dark ones preferred. On the envelope, tell the guests not to open until nightfall. Instruct them to remove the chart from the envelope, place it under a bright light for a few minutes, then turn off the lights and view the glow-in-the-dark stars and invitation information!

INVISIBLE INVITATIONS

Amaze your guests with an Invisible Invitation that seems to disappear—and appear—right before their eyes.

MATERIALS

* White construction paper
* Toothpick or fine paintbrush
* Lemon juice or milk
* Colorful felt-tip pens
* Lighter, candle, or oven
* White crayon

WHAT TO DO

Fold sheets of white construction paper in half to make cards for all the guests. Dip a toothpick repeatedly into lemon juice or milk to write the birthday information on the inside of the card. You won't be able to see what you've written, so don't forget to include all the party details! On the outside of the invitation, write "Invisible Invitation" in felt-tip pen. Underneath that, write the following instructions if using lemon juice: *Open the invitation and with a parent's supervision, carefully hold the inside of the invitation over a candle flame or a lighter.* If using milk, write: *"Bake" the invitation in a warm oven for a few minutes, until writing appears.* Or simply use a white crayon to write the party details on the white paper, and write: *Color over the inside of the invitation to make the message appear.* Don't forget to write the guests' addresses in *visible* ink!

MAGIC WANDS

Birthday parties are magical, so why not invite your guests with a Magic Wand invitation? It's sure to turn everybody into party people!

MATERIALS

* Tagboard or card-stock paper
* Gold or silver spray paint
* Glitter, metallic confetti, sequins
* 2-foot wooden dowel for each guest
* 2-foot piece of ribbon for each guest
* Small bells
* Felt-tip pens
* Scissors, glue, stapler

WHAT TO DO

For each guest, cut out a star shape from the tagboard and spray paint it with gold or silver

paint. Before the paint dries, sprinkle with glitter, metallic confetti, or sequins. Allow to dry. Write the party details on each star. Staple each star to a wooden dowel. Tie a piece of ribbon to each dowel, just under the star. Attach a small bell at the end of the ribbon. Mail in long rectangular boxes or large padded envelopes filled with confetti, or hand-deliver to guests.

MAGICAL INVITATIONS

With a little prestidigitation, you can watch these magical invitations appear before your very eyes! They're perfect for magic parties, puzzle parties, or any kind of creative party.

MATERIALS

* Inexpensive magic trick or puzzle for each guest (available at the toy store or magic shop)
* Deck of cards
* Permanent felt-tip pens

WHAT TO DO

Remove the solution sheets from the magic tricks or puzzles, leaving the guests to figure them out on their own. For each trick or puzzle, remove two or three cards from the deck of cards. On one card, write information on how to obtain the solution to the magic trick or puzzle—"Come to my party!" Add the party details to the remaining card or cards. Include the cards with the tricks or puzzles and place in padded envelopes to mail to guests. Ask the guests to bring along their magic tricks and puzzles to perform for the other guests.

MASQUERADE DISGUISES

Disguise your party details with this masquerade invitation. It's fun to make and fun for the guests to wear to the party! You can also buy inexpensive masks at a costume store to decorate as you wish.

MATERIALS

* Inexpensive store-bought mask for each guest or tagboard, string, hole punch, and gummed reinforcement holes
* Colorful felt-tip pens
* Sequins, glitter, feathers, ribbon, decals, stickers, puffy paints, and other decorations

WHAT TO DO

If not using store-bought masks, cut the tagboard to size, punch holes for string on either side of the mask and reinforce with gummed holes. Insert string and tie securely on both ends.

For both the homemade and store-bought masks, write the party details on the inside of each mask using felt-tip pens. On the outside, decorate with sequins, glitter, ribbon, feathers, or other materials. Place each mask in a padded envelope and mail to guests.

If you prefer, send the masks plain, with only the party information written on the inside. Ask the guests to decorate their own masks and wear them to the party. You can include the decorations inside the envelope, or leave it up to them. Award prizes for the best mask, funniest mask, and the scariest mask.

MUSIC! MUSIC! MUSIC!

There's music in the mailbox, when you send one of these invitations to your party guests. Here are three ways you can tune in your friends to a good time!

MATERIALS

* Sheet music
* White correction fluid
* Old record album for each guest or black tagboard

* Scissors
* Silver felt-tip pens or puffy paints
* Blank cassette tapes for each guest
* Cassette recorder

WHAT TO DO

One way to invite your friends is to use sheet music personalized for the party. Find a sheet of music and cover over the title and the lyrics using white correction fluid. Rename the song so it's appropriate to the party, such as "Fifties Sock Hop," "Rock 'n' Roll Rave," or "Matt's Bitchin' Birthday Party." Fill in the lyric lines with party details, rhyming, if possible, for added fun. Mail to guests.

Collect some old long-playing albums at a garage sale, flea market, or thrift store. (Alternatively, make "records" out of black tagboard.) Write the name of the birthday child and a song title in a circle around each disk using a silver pen or puffy paints. Insert the album into its cover and write the party details on the outside. Hand deliver to guests or mail in padded envelopes reinforced with cardboard.

Or tape record your birthday invitation! Play some party music in the background using a disk-jockey-like voice, and invite your guests to the celebration. Rewind the tapes before placing in small padded envelopes to mail to guests.

MYSTERY MESSAGES

Make your invitations a mystery challenge by sending the guests secret-coded messages they have to decipher. When they finish the translation, they're in for a big surprise—it's a party!

MATERIALS

* Codes
* Construction paper
* Black felt-tip pen

WHAT TO DO

Borrow some code books from the library and pick out a code, such as Morse Code or naval flags, or pick out a foreign language or Braille or sign language to write out. You might prefer to create your own secret code using shapes, scrambled alphabet letters, pictures, rebuses, or hieroglyphics, for example. On a practice sheet of paper, write down the party details, then translate the information into code. Cut out a large question mark from construction paper for each guest. Copy the coded party information onto the question marks. Include the key to the code in the envelope—or better yet, wait a day and then send it along! Don't give any other instructions—let the guests figure out the mystery message for themselves! To make it even more mysterious, cut the invitation into five or six pieces and send a piece each day!

NEWSPAPER HEADLINE

Paste up your own edition of the *Birthday Party News,* with the invitation as the headline.

MATERIALS

* Typewriter or computer
* White paper
* Old newspapers
* Scissors, glue, tape

WHAT TO DO

Type up the details of your party on the white paper and make enough copies for each guest. Cut and paste the typewritten invitation on to the front page of a newspaper. If you like, write more copy for the rest of the paper, using funny and bizarre stories you have read or made up. Type up headlines and sidebars, or draw cartoons to add, sized to fit the columns' length and width. Then photocopy the paste-up, one for each guest, and wrap it around the inner pages of a real newspaper before mailing.

PARTY MENUS

Invite your guests to see what's on the menu at your birthday party, using these Party Menus.

MATERIALS

* White tagboard or card-stock paper
* Computer or
* Colorful felt-tip pens
* Magazines

WHAT TO DO

Using a real restaurant menu as a model, create your own invitations to look like menus from a diner, a drive-in, a cafe, or a fancy restaurant. Name the restaurant after the birthday child and include the "daily specials," along with the party details inside. List the party food selections, along with some silly items that are not really being offered, such as octopus, chocolate-covered ants, liver, and cat food, to make it funny. Mail to guests in large envelopes and have them call to make a "reservation."

PICTURE POSTCARDS

Send your guests on a party vacation with postcard invitations! Make the postcards yourself, or pick up a collection from the travel or drugstore.

MATERIALS

* Old or new postcard or a 3 × 5-inch index card and color picture of a far-away destination, for each guest
* Scissors, glue

* Magazines
* Felt-tip pens
* Fancy stamps from the post office

WHAT TO DO

Gather an old, or buy a new, postcard for each guest. Or make postcards from blank white or colored index cards: Cut out photographs of foreign places or other unusual pictures from magazines and glue on to one side of each index card. Turn the cards over and draw a line in pencil down the middle of each card. Write the party details on the left side and the name and address of the guest on the right. Using a black felt-tip pen, write phrases on the homemade or store-bought postcards such as "Going to have a wonderful time," "Hope you'll be here!" or "I am here! You will be too!" Use a fancy stamp to send the postcards on their way!

PIRATE'S MAP

This Pirate's Map invitation shows the guests exactly where the party treasure is buried—"X"

marks the spot . . . at your house! And your swashbuckling guests can use the mailing tube as a telescope to scout for land.

MATERIALS

* Yellow or cream-colored construction paper
* Colorful felt-tip pens
* Candle or lighter
* Tape
* Chocolate coins in gold foil, foreign coins, or fake jewelry

* Cardboard tube for each guest (left over from wrapping paper or paper towels)
* Gold or black spray paint

WHAT TO DO

Cut the construction paper into large, uneven rectangles. With a felt-tip pen, draw a map for each guest to the party house from their house. Mark the party site with a large "X" or pirate flag. Add funny landmarks along the way, such as "Ye Olde McDonald's" or "Burned-Down School House." Add other details, such as "Come to Matt's Pirate Ship," with the date and time to look like clues to the destination. If you like, ask the guests to come dressed as pirates or sailors. When you're finished, wrinkle the invitation, then smooth it out and, with a parent's help, carefully burn the edges with a lighted candle or lighter to make it look old. Tape a chocolate coin at the marked "X", then roll up, and insert into the cardboard tube. Tape the ends securely and spray paint the tube gold. Let dry, then detail with black permanent felt-tip pen to look like a telescope. Address one to each guest, and mail or hand deliver. On the invitation, tell guests the mailing tube is really a pirate's telescope.

POGS

Here's a new way to invite your party guests that will delight and surprise them—use Pogs! What are Pogs? They're bottle-cap-sized disks the kids collect and use for a Tiddly-Wink-like game. Have the kids bring their Pogs to the party and play a game of Pog!

MATERIALS

* Inexpensive store-bought Pogs or heavy tagboard
* Stickers or decals
* Felt-tip pens

WHAT TO DO

Buy a number of Pogs at the toy, drug, or discount store, approximately 4 or 5 for each guest. Or make your own by using a store-bought Pog as a model for size, and cutting out circles from heavy tagboard. Cover the home-made Pogs with stickers or decals on one side, or just decorate them with felt-tip pens. Write the party details on the backs of the Pogs. For example, on one Pog write the date and time of the party. On a second, write the host's name and address. On a third, write the type of party you're hosting. And on the fourth, write additional information, such as what to wear or bring, for example. Slip the Pogs into an envelope and mail to your guests.

POPCORN PARTY BAGS

What a treat to find a bag of popcorn in the mailbox, especially when there's a party invitation along with it.

MATERIALS

* Striped paper popcorn bags or paper lunch bags
* Felt-tip pens, stickers, puffy paints
* Popped popcorn
* Ribbon

WHAT TO DO

Buy popcorn bags or decorate lunch bags with felt-tip pens, stickers, and puffy paints. Pop popcorn and fill the bags. Place a note listing the party details in each bag, then secure the bags closed with ribbon. Hand deliver to guests.

POPPERS

Give the guests an invitation with a surprise inside! You can make your Poppers look like firecrackers or giant candies. Or use your imagination for other possibilities.

MATERIALS

* Toy or treat related to the birthday theme, for each guest
* Confetti
* Red tissue paper
* Toilet paper roll for each guest
* Red crepe paper
* Ribbon
* Scissors

* Sparkly pipe cleaners
* Permanent felt-tip pen

WHAT TO DO

Pick out a toy or treat that relates to the party theme, such as a harmonica, trading card, or pack of gum. Using felt-tip pen, write the party details on the toy or treat, if possible, or write them on a small note and attach. Pour some confetti on to a sheet of red tissue paper, place the toy or treat on top, and wrap up, twisting the ends closed. Stuff into the toilet paper roll. Wrap with red crepe paper and tie off ends with ribbon. Fringe the ends with scissors, add a sparkly pipe cleaner to one end to make a fire-cracker, or decorate it to look like a piece of giant candy. Mail in boxes or padded envelopes to guests.

POP-UP CARDS

For eye-popping fun, have your invitations pop out in 3-D by following the instructions below.

MATERIALS

* Construction paper
* Glue, scissors, tape
* Felt-tip pens
* 3-D pictures

WHAT TO DO

With a pencil, sketch your home, a castle, a haunted mansion, or other structure on a sheet of construction paper. Draw on several doors and windows, and cut them along three sides so they will open. Go over the design in felt-tip pen, adding detail to your building. Glue this sheet to a piece of different colored construction paper , being careful not to glue down the doors and windows. Fold open the doors and windows and write the party details under the flaps. Close the flaps and seal with stickers or tape. Mail to guests in large envelopes.

Or make a giant mouth that offers party details pop out of the invitation. Fold a sheet of construction paper in half. Make a cut on the fold in the center in the shape of a "V," leaving the tip of the V intact. Open the fold and press the V fold in the opposite direction, so it comes out toward you. Cut out a smaller V inside the large V and remove it to make the mouth opening. Draw a head around the mouth and a speech bubble to write the party details in.

Or make 3-D invitations using popular 3-D pictures. Buy an inexpensive paperback version of the 3-D image books. Tear out the pages (or photocopy them) and write the party details around the edges of the pictures. Mail to guests, enclosing a brief explanation of how to make the 3-D image appear (instructions are in the books).

PUZZLERS

These Puzzlers must be assembled by your guests before they can be read. Here are three ways you can make these intriguing puzzle invitations.

MATERIALS

* Tagboard
* Map
* Spray adhesive
* Wooden ice cream sticks
* Felt-tip pens, crayons, or paint
* Masking tape, scissors

WHAT TO DO

For one way to puzzle your friends, write the party details on one side of sheets of tagboard. Fill up the whole side with words, pictures, and designs—all relating to the party's theme. Cut each tagboard into puzzle shapes. Place shapes into small envelopes and mail to guests. Let them figure out how to put the puzzle together so they can read the invitation. To make it even harder, write on both sides of the tagboard!

A map to the party house is another puzzling way to invite your friends. Buy a map of your community and make a photocopy for each guest of the section featuring the party destination. Mark the path from each guest's house to your house with felt-tip pen, write the party details around the outside or on the back, then glue the map onto tagboard using spray adhesive. Cut up into puzzle pieces and mail to guests.

Or buy ice cream sticks, five or six for each guest. Lay them side by side and tape them together at the top and bottom with masking tape. Write the party details on one side of the sticks. Turn the sticks over and color with crayon, felt-tip pen, or paint. Pull off the tape and drop the sticks into an envelope with instructions to put the puzzle sticks together to make the invitation.

RECIPE CARDS

Write down all the ingredients you need for a perfect party on your Recipe Cards and mail them to the guests so they can cook up some fun!

MATERIALS

* Recipe cards or index cards
* Felt-tip pens or stickers
* A favorite recipe
* Some of the ingredients used in the recipe
* Finished product (optional)

WHAT TO DO

Buy ready-made blank recipe cards, or decorate index with felt-tip pens or stickers. On the cards, write a favorite recipe, such as chocolate chip cookies, cupcakes, chocolate shakes, or anything you like. Place a recipe card for each guest in a padded envelope or small box along with some of the ingredients called for in the recipe, such as chocolate chips, tubes of frosting, sprinkles, or chocolate powder. Include a sample of the final product, if possible. Hand deliver or mail to guests to whet their appetites for the party!

SWIRL STICKS

Swirl Stick invitations give the kids something to play with after they've read the party details!

MATERIALS

* 4- to 6-foot length of crepe paper streamer or colorful fabric for each guest
* Felt-tip pen
* Stickers and glitter
* 1-foot wooden dowel for each guest
* Masking tape, scissors

WHAT TO DO

Write the party details along the length of the crepe paper or piece of fabric. Decorate with stickers and glitter. Tape one end of the banner to the dowel and roll the crepe paper or fabric around the stick. Secure the end with a sticker, tape, or rubber band. Place in padded envelopes or small boxes and mail to guests, or hand deliver. Ask them to bring their Swirl Sticks to the party, then have everyone wave them in the air to make patterns and designs!

THIS IS YOUR LIFE!

This personalized invitation can be used for any birthday party theme. The focus is on the spe-cial birthday child, but it works especially well with the "This Is Your Life!" party.

MATERIALS

* Pictures of birthday child as a baby and today, with others in between, if desired
* Sheets of 8 $\frac{1}{2}$ × 11-inch construction paper
* Glitter, sequins, puffy paints
* Gummed corners, glue, or cellophane
* Ribbon
* Hole punch
* Felt-tip pens

WHAT TO DO

Take your child's photographs to the copy store and make enough copies of each one for all the guests. Fold construction paper in half to make a card. On the front of the card, write "This Is Your Life!" and the birthday child's name. Decorate the outside with glitter, sequins, and puffy paints. Trim the photocopied photographs of your child. Arrange one pair inside the card invitation, with the baby picture on the left and the current pic-ture on the right. Secure photos with gummed corners, glue, or tape to make a mini-photo album. Add more pages and more pictures of the birthday child over the years, if you like. Write party details below the pictures, reminding the guests that the party theme is a surprise. On the back of the card, cut out a black silhouette of an expected surprise guest, and draw black question marks all around the outline to add to the mystery. Punch a hole in the card and decorate with ribbon. Mail to guests. For fun, ask them all to come dressed as the birthday child!

TICKET TO FUN

All the guests need for admittance to your party is a Ticket to Fun invitation! Here's one you can make that's guaranteed to save a place for your special friends. That's the ticket!

MATERIALS

* Colorful card-stock paper or index cards
* Scissors, hole punch
* Fine-point permanent black felt-tip pen
* Gummed stars, glitter, stickers

WHAT TO DO

Cut card-stock paper into rectangles the size of 3 × 5-inch index cards. Use a hole punch to create a perforated ticket edge. Use a real ticket as a guide for writing your party details, such as "Admit One . . . to a Party!" Decorate with gummed stars, glitter, or stickers, and insert in an envelope.

If you prefer, buy a roll of tickets from a party store, tear off a length, and write the party details on top of the tickets. On the back, write the guests names, then have them bring the tickets to the party for a surprise drawing.

UNIDENTIFIED FLYING OBJECTS

Heads up! This UFO is coming in for a landing. And it makes a great toy, too!

MATERIALS

* Construction paper
* Felt-tip pens

* Staples or tape
* Stickers and decals

WHAT TO DO

Using your favorite paper airplane design, or following the directions in a paper airplane book from the library, create enough paper planes for all your guests. Open up the folded planes and write the party details in spaces that won't show when the airplane is refolded. Write in the age of the child as the flight number, fill in the "arrival" and "departure" times, and don't forget the "destination." Then refold the airplane, staple or tape the bottom closed, decorate with stickers and decals, or felt-tip pens, and slip into an envelope. If you prefer, make the invitations out of pre-cut balsa wood airplanes, and write your party details on the plane parts. Let the guests put the airplanes together. Happy landing!

WANTED POSTERS

Visit the post office for a look at a real Wanted Poster, then create your own, featuring the birthday child as one of the FBI's Most Wanted. Offer birthday stats instead of the typical criminal information, and mail to guests or tack to a tree outside their homes.

MATERIALS

* Sheets of colored construction paper
* Large head shot of birthday child
* Felt-tip pens
* Tape, glue, tacks

WHAT TO DO

Make a photocopy of a large head shot of your child for each guest. Glue or tape the photocopy to sheets of construction paper to make a frame. Write the party details in the form of a Wanted Poster, such as "Wanted for a Party" and "Last Seen Wearing a Party Hat" and "REWARD!" with party date and time. Mail to guests in large envelopes or tack them to their front doors or trees outside their homes.

DELIGHTFUL DECORATIONS

You can create an entire party backdrop with just a little imagination and a few easily obtained materials. Using crepe paper, construction paper, cardboard, posters, streamers, fancy lighting, creative cut-outs, paints, and felt-tip pens, you can transform the family room into a fantasy land, the backyard into a beach, or the garage into a Jurassic jungle.

Inexpensive art materials are a colorful and economical way to convert your party room into a paradise. Cut construction paper into tall trees to tack on the walls. Make colorful rainbows to spread across the ceiling. Or fill the "sky" with clouds, stars, spaceships, or birds. Add posters, banners, streamers, balloons, and you've got a party!

If you aren't creative with paper and paint, pick up a few ready-made items at the store and distribute them around the room. You might decorate with small dolls, picture books, comic cut-outs, funny photographs, sheet music, CD or album covers, masks and costumes, magazine pictures, swaths of fabric, reproductions of artwork, large posters, or removable decals. When the party is over, send the guests home with some of the special decorations.

If outside, consider decorating any object or place for a party: bicycles, skates, a trampoline, the car or van, a tree, a tent, a park. Weave bike spokes with crepe paper streamers, apply stickers to roller skates, tie balloons to the trampoline, tape a banner to the car, or fill the tree with presents.

If inside, you can add to the whimsy of the party room by making mobiles using wire coat hangers and fishing line, and hang cut-up pictures, toys, candies, stars, toothbrushes, or other fun-to-look-at items that fit the theme.

Create bouquets and centerpieces for the party table using flowers, balloons, crepe paper, the cake, the gifts, snacks, stuffed animals, photographs of the party person and/or the guests, or other theme-related decorations.

Draw caricatures of the guests on a paper tablecloth to show them where to sit, or use photographs as place markers. Or make the tablecloth a guessing game in which the kids have to figure out where to sit using clues written on the tablecloth.

Make place mats out of burlap with the sides fringed, then place cartoons, flowers, pictures, or other flat items in the center and cover with clear Con-Tact paper. (Or let the kids make their own place mats and place markers for a party activity.) Sprinkle confetti over the tablecloth, and add stickers, pictures, colorful paper plates, small toys, or candies.

Make festive and theme-related place markers: cookies, giant lollipops, or cupcakes with the guests' names written in icing; look-alike paper dolls; small stuffed animals; pictures of the guests; pencils or rulers with the guests' names written in puffy paints; cards or paper with the guests' names cut-out or stenciled on.

Decorate the front door, garage door, and mailbox with banners, balloons, signs, candies, and crepe paper streamers to welcome the guests when they first arrive. Then spruce up the kitchen, the bathroom, and the birthday child's room, just for fun.

As soon as you're finished, simply open the doors to your party palace and welcome your guests!

ALL ABOUT YOU

Since this is a special day for the birthday child, why not decorate the party room as a shrine to the honoree! Make it a surprise if you can.

MATERIALS

* Toys from your child's room
* Favorite clothing items
* Arts and crafts made by the birthday child
* Pictures of your child from birth to the present
* Favorite foods, treats, and drinks

WHAT TO DO

Gather some special items from your child's past and present to use as decorations for the party room. Include favorite toys and dolls, baseball cards, boxed games, clothing, drawings, and paintings. Place them around the room, tack them to the walls, or hang them from the ceiling. Use some of the items to make a table centerpiece. Tape photographs of your child at various ages to sheets of colored construction paper, and tape them on the walls for everyone to see. You might write funny captions to go with each one, and later play a game where the guests have to guess how old the birthday person was in the picture. Make one blow-up picture to put at the front door to greet the guests. Go to the library and photocopy pages of the newspapers or magazines that were published on the day your child was born. Hang them on the wall to show what was happening in the world on that special day. Ask the guests to bring a memento of their friendship and have the birthday child guess what it is and what occasion it represents. Take pictures of your child's favorite places around town and put them up around the walls or on the party table, then label them with funny sayings or have everyone guess where the pictures were taken and why. Use photocopied pictures of your child covered in clear Con-Tact paper as place mats, and make a cake in the shape of a favorite toy, book, or cartoon character.

ARTIST COLONY

Offer your guests a few hours of arts and crafts at your Artist Colony retreat. Fill the party room with priceless works of arts and crafts made by the kids.

MATERIALS

* Arts and crafts supplies, such as poster paints, watercolors, finger paints, chalk, felt-tip pens, crayons, puffy paints, pencils, construction paper, card-stock paper, fancy papers, foil, fabric, glitter, sequins, confetti, stickers, glue, tape, staples, scissors
* Old sheet
* Easels
* Posters of artwork
* Masterpiece art prints to copy
* Sculptures, ceramics, and collages
* Old shirts or smocks

WHAT TO DO

Get out arts and crafts supplies and set them up on a table covered with the sheet. A few hours before the party, sprinkle paint on the sheet and allow it to dry. It will give the table an arty look. Set up easels and place art posters on them, or hang the posters on the walls. Make up some of your own posters using large sheets of white paper and paint. Copy some of the masters, create your own designs, or paint funny portraits of each of your guests. Collect other works of art, such as sculptures and ceramic pieces, and place them on the table for the centerpiece. Create and hang a large painting on the garage door to greet your guests. Set up different art areas, such as a sculpting area with clay and play dough; a wood shop area with scraps of wood, hammer, nails, and saw; a painting area, with finger paints, watercolors, and poster paints; and a cartooning area, with inspiration cartoons, colored pencils, and felt-tip pens. Give everyone an old shirt or artist's smock when they arrive at the party, and allow them to get as messy as they like.

BABY LOVE

Go back in time with a Baby Love party room, filled with infancy fun. Keep the emphasis on the party honoree alone, or include all your guests in the baby decor.

MATERIALS

* Baby pictures
* Baby food jars
* Baby clothes
* Baby toys
* Baby equipment
* Baby books
* Baby items, such as diaper pins, diapers, baby spoons, teethers, bibs
* Pink and blue construction paper
* Yellow tablecloth, pink and blue plates

WHAT TO DO

Set up the room as if it were one large baby room filled with all kinds of baby-related items. Put pictures of your birthday child on the wall, in a series from newborn to 3 years old (or make a game of it and scramble up the display. Have the kids guess how old the baby is in each picture!) Blow up some baby pictures into giant photos to hang on the walls. Get baby photos of all the kids invited to the party and display them on the walls too, then have everyone guess who's who. Or find pictures of movie stars when they were babies and put them on the walls for a guessing game. Cover the table with a yellow paper tablecloth and use pink and blue plates for food and cake. Make a centerpiece from small baby items such as baby powder, teethers, and baby spoons, or set up a collection of baby dolls. Make the cake in the shape of a large rattle, a baby T-shirt, or decorate to look like a birth certificate. Cut tiny diaper shapes from pink and blue construction paper, and larger ones for place mats. Set baby books around the room, as well as baby dolls, baby clothes, baby toys, and baby equipment. Borrow items from each of the guest's parents that have been saved from their children's baby years and display them on a special table, then have the kids guess which item belongs to which guest.

BILLIONS OF BALLOONS

A few balloons at a party are nice, but billions are better! Decorate your party world with "billions and billions" of balloons and watch the room blow up with color and cheer.

MATERIALS

* Balloons
* Ribbon
* Yarn or string
* Crepe paper
* Construction paper
* Permanent felt-tip pens

WHAT TO DO

Begin the birthday with a balloon surprise. Blow up lots of balloons and fill up the birthday child's closet, bedroom, bathroom, playhouse, or other small area with lots of balloons. If you don't have a special place to fill with balloons, get a large box from the appliance store and fill it with helium balloons. Wrap the box and set it on the front doorstep. Ring the door bell, run away, and let the birthday honoree open up the box of balloons. Decorate the party room with the "billions" of balloons. Electrify them by rubbing them on your body and sticking them to the walls. If they won't stay up, use a bit of double-stick tape. Fill the ceiling with helium balloons. You can rent a helium filler at a party or hobby store for a nominal price. Tie balloons to lengths of ribbon or string every few inches until you have a garland of balloons. Drape or swag the garlands from the center of the ceiling to the far corners.

Or make a canopy of balloons by tying the garlands around the doorway, swagging at the top. Decorate the balloons with funny faces, caricatures of your guests, or witty sayings. Add detail with permanent felt-tip pens or cut-outs from construction paper. Create arms and legs by accordion-pleating crepe paper streamers and taping them to the sides and bottom of the balloons, then float them from the ceiling.

Have all the guests bring balloon bouquets to the party and release them all over the party room at a set time. Or have a special bouquet of balloons delivered to the party. For a nice surprise, send your party guests a helium balloon through the mail wrapped in a big box and delivered by a package service.

BLAST TO THE PAST

Go back to the fifties, sixties, seventies, or eighties for a Blast To The Past party, and decorate the room in retro.

MATERIALS

* Collection of items from a favorite decade such as:
  * The fifties, when rock and roll was king, Elvis was our leader, and poodle skirts and leather jackets ruled.
  * The sixties, when hippies created the love generation, the Beatles were pop stars, and long hair and bell-bottoms were groovy.
  * The seventies, when disco took over, "Saturday Night Fever" was highly contagious, and polyester was cool.
  * The eighties, when new-wave/punk appeared, the "Me" generation was in charge, and torn clothes and spike hair were in.
  * Even the early nineties, when rap and hip-hop fought it out with alternative music, computers influenced our lives, and fashion was flannel, oversized, and grungy.

WHAT TO DO

For the fifties, you might decorate with 45 RPM records, poodle skirts, combs, pictures of cherried-up Chevies, and posters of Elvis. You might rent a jukebox for the occasion and play the Supremes, Dion and the Belmonts, and Pat Boone!

For the sixties, you'll need psychedelic posters on the walls, guitars around the room, and tie-dyed T-shirts with flower pants. Make up protest signs for the guests to carry, or tape them to the walls. Be sure to play the Beatles, the Rolling Stones, and the Grateful Dead. Burn incense for an authentic atmosphere.

The seventies were personified by the Brady Bunch, so decorate using the popular TV show in mind, with flower prints, bad hair, and the Carpenters or the Jackson Five playing in the background. Or make it a Disco party with seventies' classics, such as Donna Summer and the Bee-Gees. Make a Pac-Man cake for a centerpiece.

For the eighties, turn on the Talking Heads, Devo, and the Smiths, and have everyone dress in leather, studs, torn jeans, and mohawk wigs. Hang posters of pop stars or popular TV shows.

For the early nineties, check out magazines such as *Sassy* or *Dirt;* TV shows such as *Ninja Turtles* or the *Power Rangers;* or musical groups such as Pearl Jam or Boyz II Men for ideas. Don't forget to include wall displays, music, and food to match.

CAFE PARTEE

Open your own stylized cafe to host your birthday party and use your dining room as the party room!

MATERIALS

* Old sheets or blankets
* One large table or several small card tables
* Fancy tablecloths
* Fancy silverware, dishes, glasses, and cloth napkins
* Menus
* Candles
* Mood music

WHAT TO DO

If possible, section off the dining room or party room by hanging sheets or blankets across the doorway openings, so the room is cozy, intimate, and cut off from the rest of the house. Set up a large table or several card tables in the room and cover them with fancy tablecloths, place mats, and table settings. Use your best dishes or dishes to suit the theme of the party. Fold the cloth napkins in a fancy design and set them at each plate. Make place cards at each table using an idea from the party theme, or make them elegant, using black paper with white ink. Make menus for each guest, beginning with appetizers to soup or salad, main course, vegetable or side dish, dessert, and drinks. Offer the kids a couple of choices if you have them, and make all the other choices silly, like "peanut butter and banana sandwich" or "lima bean pate." Light the candles and turn on the mood music. When the guests begin to arrive, take their coats and show them into the secluded dining area. Serve the drinks in fancy champagne or wine glasses, with bubbles, a cherry, and a small paper umbrella. When everyone has arrived, offer them menus, then take their orders on a pad. Dress in black and white to look like a waiter and serve the meal in courses. Present them with the outrageous bill at the end of the evening, but don't expect a tip.

CANDY LAND

What child wouldn't want to visit Candy Land for a few hours? Turn your party room into a child's garden of tasty delights!

MATERIALS

* Candy—all sorts, shapes, flavors, and sizes
* Candy-related items, such as games, T-shirts, books
* Tagboard and construction paper

WHAT TO DO

First decorate the front door: On a sheet of heavy tagboard, glue or tape down individually wrapped hard candies in a variety of colors and flavors. Arrange them in an attractive design, or write Happy Birthday with the candies, then allow glue to dry. Tack the candy-covered tagboard to the front door to welcome the guests as they arrive, and let them help themselves to the door treats on the way home. Decorate the walls with candies, or pictures of candies clipped from food magazines. Drape streamers of lollipops in the doorways to use as a screen separating one room from another, or use them as swags from the center of the ceiling to the far corners. Have the kids enter the room following an enlarged "Candy Land" route, then play a giant game of Candy Land during the party, using construction paper spaces and real candies to move the players along their way. Cover the tablecloth with tiny loose candies, such as Red Hots, miniature M & Ms, cake-decorating candies. Make a small "house" out of a cardboard box and cover with small candies. Hide chocolate coins throughout the party room for the kids to find and eat. (You might want to have a race to see who finds the most chocolate coins.) Get pictures of the kids and make cardboard frames to hold their photographs. Decorate the frames with candies and use them as place markers.

CARNIVAL BOOTHS

Set up a carnival in your backyard or garage and turn your party into a homemade circus. Decorate the cardboard booths with paint and crepe paper, tie balloons around the room, and hang up large posters of clowns and creative cut-outs of animals to add to the carnival atmosphere.

MATERIALS

* Large cardboard boxes to use as booths
* Posters, streamers, ribbons, balloons
* Construction paper and other arts and crafts materials
* Poster paints and felt-tip pens in a variety of colors
* garden hose
* 3 hula hoops

WHAT TO DO

Large cardboard boxes can be found at appliance stores. Paint the boxes with different colors of poster paint and allow to dry. Cut out holes in the boxes to create booths for games, such as penny pitching, ring the bottle, baseball toss, clothes pin drop, coin on a plate, fishing rod, and bowling throw. Cut out several more boxes to serve as popcorn, candy, and ticket sales booths. Have booths that offer face-painting, fortune-telling, tarot-reading, and fake tattooing. Create a carnival big top by swagging different colors of crepe paper streamers from the ceiling to the floor. Hang posters of clowns and animals. Make clown faces on balloons and hang them from ceiling. Set out all your big stuffed animals behind "bars," in cages cut from large cardboard boxes, or have a friend dress up as a wild animal and snarl from the cage. Use a hose to make a large ring around three hula hoops and feature special circus acts in the rings. Play circus music, add twinkling holiday lights, and have parent helpers come dressed as clowns.

CASBAH CANOPY

It's amazing what you do can do with yards and yards of crepe paper streamers, a few balloons, and some fabric. Turn your party room into a Casbah Canopy, and invite your guests to the exotic location for an atmospheric party.

MATERIALS

* Rolls of crepe paper in a variety of colors
* Pillows

WHAT TO DO

Clear the room of furniture, if possible. Using rolls of crepe paper, tape one end to the top of one wall and twist a length down to the floor, and tape to the bottom of the wall. Repeat along all four walls, placing one crepe paper row right next to another until the whole room is covered with crepe paper. Cover the ceiling with a swag of crepe paper streamers, starting from the center of the ceiling to the outsides, until the whole ceiling is covered. Ask the kids to bring their pillows to the party, and collect ones you have around the house. Set pillows in the center of the room, dim the lights, turn on some exotic music, and have your party under the Casbah Canopy.

COMIC-CARTOON TOWN

Welcome the kids to your very own Toon Town. With a little help from your favorite animated characters, you'll soon be in a fantasy birthday world.

MATERIALS

* Sunday funnies
* Construction paper
* Comic books
* Cartoon character figurines
* Coloring books
* Disney posters

WHAT TO DO

Save the Sunday funny papers and cut out your favorite comic strips. Mount them on construction paper backgrounds and decorate the walls with them. For fun, white-out the speech balloons with correction fluid and add your own funny sayings. Personalize them by referring to the guests. Or cut them up into individual panels, scramble them up, and place them on the table for guests to put in the correct order. Buy comic books and place them all around the party room. Or tear them up into individual sheets and use the pages as place mats, table decorations, or wall hangings. Set little plastic cartoon characters on the tables as decorations, then pass them out as favors. Or hang them from the ceiling, or make them into necklaces and give them to the guests to wear during the party, then take home. Use coloring books, posters, trading cards, or inexpensive cartoon picture books to turn your room into a Toon Town. Give the kids Mickey Mouse ears or cartoon shirts to wear. Be sure to play cartoon music in the background.

DISNEYROOM

Make a trip to a Disneyroom—right in your own home! Invite Mickey and Donald and all the gang to join your friends at party time.

MATERIALS

* Disney items, such as posters, figures, T-shirts, books, tapes, videos
* Disney paper products for the birthday party

WHAT TO DO

Collect as many Disney-related products as you can, and ask your guests to bring some too. Decorate the walls with posters or pages of Disney picture books, play Disney audio and video tapes, place Disney figurines around the room, and set up the Disney table with a Disney tablecloth. Have the kids dress as characters from Disney films to add to the atmosphere. Set up different areas of the house or room as different areas in Disneyland. Decorate "Fantasy Land" with cartoon characters; "Frontier Land" with lots of western stuff; "Adventure Land" with a jungle motif; and "Tomorrow Land" with posters, pictures, and props that have an outer-space theme. Give the kids tickets as they enter the party, or send the tickets as invitations. Create "rides" and "adventures" in each section of the party room.

ENCHANTED FOREST

Take the kids into a magical, Enchanted Forest, where special creatures live and strange things happen. All you need are construction materials and lots of imagination.

MATERIALS

* A variety pack of colored construction paper
* A pack of green construction paper
* A pack of brown construction paper
* A variety of crepe paper or tissue paper colors
* Large sheets of green and blue crepe paper
* Large cardboard boxes or sections of cardboard
* Brown and green poster paint
* Glow-in-the-dark paint
* Paintbrushes, scissors, glue, tape

WHAT TO DO:

Cut out brown construction paper to make tree trunks and tape the trunks all around the walls of the party room. Cut out green paper to make tree tops to tape above the trunks. Use cardboard that has been painted brown and green to make three-dimensional trees to set around the forest. Cut out small squares of green crepe paper and squish them lightly into balls. Glue or tape them to the tree tops to make three-dimensional leaves. Use large sheets of green crepe paper to swag around ceiling, to make dense forest. Add a strip or two of blue crepe paper in the center of the ceiling to make night sky, and dot with glow-in-the-dark paint to make sparkling stars. Cut out black circles from construction paper and paint with glow-in-the-dark paint to make glowing eyes. Tape eyes to trees to give a feeling of being watched. Cut out colored construction paper and wrinkle up colored crepe paper to form colorful flowers in the forest. Tape or glue them in clusters to the base of the tree trunks. Using construction paper, draw and cut out animals such as owls, deer, and rabbits, and place them around the forest, peeking out from behind tree leaves and trunks. Play a sound-effects tape of forest sounds for background atmosphere.

MELODY LAND

A music-lover's party offers lots of opportunities for decorating ideas. Whether it's country or punk, hip-hop or rock, create a Melody Land to suit the musical theme.

MATERIALS

* Album and CD covers
* Tapes and CDs
* Posters and postcards of music stars
* White and black poster board
* Felt-tip pens

WHAT TO DO

Find old record covers at thrift stores, or use your favorite CD covers to decorate the walls and table. Play popular tapes and CDs in the background. Tape up posters on the walls of favorite music singers or groups, and set postcards of rock stars at the table as place markers. Write familiar lines from famous or popular songs on white poster board and hang them from the ceiling or place on the walls and table. Or cut the white poster board into in the musical note shapes to hang around the room. Cut out the black poster board in the shape of record albums and 45s and write in funny song titles performed by your guests. Hang them on the walls or use them as place mats. Make a sheet cake and decorate it to look like a cassette tape. Dress like a favorite musician.

MYSTERY MANSION

Offer lots of mysterious surprises to your party guests at your Mystery Mansion birthday. Everything from the invitations to the favors should be mysterious . . .

MATERIALS

* Small boxes filled with a surprise inside, such as a toy or candy
* Blank puzzle pieces
* Codes
* Construction paper

WHAT TO DO

After sending your guests Mystery Messages (page 79) they have to put together or decode, prepare the party room for more mystery and intrigue. Have someone answer the door in disguise and don't let the party guests know who the mysterious stranger is until the party is over—just keep them guessing. Then make it a big surprise by revealing a favorite teacher, coach, group leader, or local celebrity. Cut out question marks of all sizes and colors from construction paper. Tape them all over the party room—on the walls, the table, the furniture, the floors, and hang them from the ceiling using black thread. Wrap up the favors in fancy boxes and hang them from the ceiling. Let the guests choose a mystery box, then open it to find their thank-you-for-coming gift. Write their names on place markers in code. Give them decoders so they can figure out their places at the table. Or set the table with place markers in the shape of question marks and give clues as to who sits at each place. Let the guests sit down when they have figured out where they belong. Serve mystery food (such as combined soups) and a mystery cake with a surprise ingredient (a toy baked right inside!).

PARALLEL UNIVERSE

Your Parallel Universe can serve as a backdrop for a number of parties, where things are familiar—yet different. You can make everything upside down, backwards, or slightly "off," depending on your theme. Are the guests sitting at the table real, or are they Cloned Companions from a Parallel Universe party? That's for your friends to figure out when they arrive—from another dimension.

MATERIALS

* Child-size lengths of butcher paper, 2 per person
* Polyester fiberfill
* Staples, tape, glue
* Felt-tip pens
* Old clothes from your guests, if possible
* Photographs of your guests

* Toys, hobbies, books, and tapes from your guests

WHAT TO DO

Secretly contact your guests' parents and make arrangements ahead of time: Collect an outfit, some toys, stuffed animals, tapes, or books, and a large picture of each guest, which you will return. Photocopy the pictures of your guests, in color if possible, or color them when you are finished photocopying. Have the birthday child lie down on a sheet of white butcher paper and outline the body; repeat for the number of guests two times, each pair in the same position. Cut out on outline. Draw details of face and hands on the body with felt-tip pens, making each body outline look like one of the guests. Staple to a second body outline, leaving an opening at one side, then stuff with polyester fiberfill to give it a 3-D look. Staple the tops and bottoms closed. Dress the clones in old clothes you have borrowed secretly from guests' homes. Set them at the table, around the party room on the chairs and couch, or tack them to the walls to make them look like they are standing.

To make place mats, glue photocopied pictures of guests to sheets of construction paper and cover with clear Con-Tact paper. Set guest's toys, games, and other items around the party room and on the table as a centerpiece. Then surprise your guests as they arrive in your Parallel Universe.

SPIDER'S DEN

"Welcome to my web," said the spider to the fly. Create your own spider web decorations if you want to catch a whole bunch of party guests!

MATERIALS

* Black yarn
* Tacks or tape
* White webbing (from the craft store) or polyester fiberfill batting (from the fabric store)

WHAT TO DO

Welcome your unsuspecting guests at the door with a giant spider web. Using black yarn, begin

the web by tacking or taping down one end of the yarn from the top of the door to the bottom. Continue running yarn from one end to the other, moving it a foot away from the last tack in a circular pattern, until you have covered the front door with yarn that looks like a giant spider web. Leave an opening in the middle as you weave your web so the kids can wiggle through to get into the party. Hang rubber spiders all over the web, then invite your guests inside through the hole. Once inside, create a maze of webbing using the black yarn. With one end of the yarn, begin at one point in the room and tack the yarn into place. Move to another part of the room, winding the yarn over and under furniture, back and forth, here and there, until the room is completely covered in webbing. Have the kids try to crawl through the yarn maze from one side of the room to the other, or crawl through the maze without touching any yarn, or follow a piece of yarn from beginning to end. Or create one web path for each guest. Have them start at one end of the yarn and follow it all the way to the other end, where there's a prize waiting for them. Add touches of white webbing throughout the party room, by pulling apart fiberfill and taping it to the corners of the walls, furniture, and doors.

SPOOKY CAVE

Kids love to creep around in spooky places, like caves, mines, tunnels, and forts. Create a scary setting for your birthday party in a Spooky Cave.

MATERIALS

* Large cardboard boxes
* Card tables

* Long poles or sticks
* Black paint
* Large sheets or blankets
* Glow-in-the-dark stickers
* Flashlights
* Rubber spiders, rats, and bats

WHAT TO DO

Bring home some large boxes from your local appliance stores. Lay them on their sides and cut large openings on both ends of the boxes. Arrange the boxes opening-to-opening, or turning here and there, to create a tunnel. Paint the inside black, add glitter to make it sparkle, and hang rubber spiders and hide rubber rats in the tunnel. Stick on glow-in-the-dark stickers. Let the kids crawl in or through the boxes and have some of the party inside the dark tunnel. Or borrow several card tables from friends and neighbors and set them up in the party room. Cover with sheets or blankets and let the kids have their party in the cave. Turn off the lights and give everyone a flashlight to shine in the dark. Or simply rearrange the furniture in one room to create a fortress or cave, by laying long sticks or poles across the tops of the furniture and covering everything up with sheets and blankets. Let the kids go inside the cave to have the party. For best effects, have the party at night.

STARRY, STARRY NIGHT

There's nothing like a starry night to give your party atmosphere. Here's a way to make the night sky a shining delight.

MATERIALS

* Glow-in-the-dark paint, pens, stickers, and stars
* Constellation charts or books
* Old sheets
* Tagboard
* Black thread
* Black T-shirts

WHAT TO DO

Host your party at night so your guests will really see stars when they arrive. Using constellation charts as a guide, paint or stick on stars and planets all over the ceiling. Decorate the walls, too, with stickers that can be peeled off later, or paint stars on old sheets to hang on the walls. Cut out stars, planets, moons, and space ships from tagboard. Paint them with the glow-in-the-dark paint. Attach black thread and hang from the ceiling at different lengths. Paint star designs or guest's names on black T-shirts with glow-in-the-dark fabric paint. Shine a light over all the glow-in-the-dark items, turn off the lights, and watch the room come to light.

TENT SAFARI

Turn the backyard into a jungle and have a Tent Safari in the dark.

MATERIALS

* Tent or rope, blanket, tarp, and large stones
* Sleeping bags
* Flashlights

* Logs or barbecue
* White construction paper
* Glow-in-the-dark paint and brushes
* Felt-tip pens and stapler
* Tape recorder and cassette tape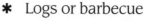
* Comic books
* Backpacks, canteens, compasses

WHAT TO DO

For a party in the wilderness (but not too far from home) first pitch a tent. You can use a real tent—a large one or several small ones. Or you can make your own homemade tent: Tie a rope between two trees and toss a blanket over the rope. Lay a tarp on the ground under the blanket, and secure the blanket corners with large stones. Have the kids bring sleeping bags, and give them each a flashlight (or ask them to bring one). Set up a safe campfire by laying logs on a barbecue grill under adult supervision, or just use the hibachi or barbecue as your campfire. To give your backyard a jungle atmosphere, cut out stars from the white construction paper and paint them with glow-in-the-dark paint, then staple them up in the trees. Then cut out circles or ovals for eyes, and paint them with glow-in-the-dark paint, adding black dots in the center for the pupils. Staple them in pairs to trees, to the fence, and around the yard, so when it gets dark they will glow like the eyes of animals, hiding in the bushes. Draw pictures of animals, such as owls, bears, or snakes, and set them around the yard to add to the feeling of a wilderness. Tape record animal sounds made by you or by real animals, or play a tape that has animal sounds on it, and hide the tape recorder in the bushes. Play it when everyone goes to bed.

TREASURE ISLAND

What could be better than being trapped on a deserted island for a birthday party! Welcome your guests to Treasure Island for an afternoon of fun in the sun.

MATERIALS

* Sandbox
* Kiddy pool
* Balloons
* Sand and water toys
* Tiki torches or colored lights
* Construction paper
* Tropical posters
* Tropical music
* Cardboard box
* Brown paint
* Fake jewels, inexpensive necklaces, and other play jewelry
* Chocolate coins in gold foil
* Coconuts, pineapples, and other tropical fruits
* White sheets and sticks
* Felt-tip pens

WHAT TO DO

Head for the beach for an authentic Treasure Island setting. Or create your own in the backyard, on the patio, or in the garage. Set out a sandbox and kiddy pool if you can't go to the beach. Blow up balloons and draw fish and shark faces on them. Toss them into the water or hang them from a fence. Place sand and water toys around for the kids to enjoy, such as pails, sifters, shovels, water guns, and beach balls. Decorate the party area with Tiki torches or colored lights, by securing them around fences or trees. Use construction paper to cut out large fish, tropical flowers, coral designs, and shells, and place around the party area. Hang up tropical posters, and play Hawaiian or Polynesian music in the background. Ask the guests to dress for the beach or the island, in swimsuits, towels, shorts, and tops. Decorate the table with shells, suntan lotion, sunglasses, sand pails, or with tropical fruit, such as coconuts and pineapples. Feature a sheet cake topped with brown sugar to look like a sandy beach. Paint a cardboard box to look like a treasure chest, glue on fake jewels, and fill with chocolate gold coins and inexpensive necklaces for discovered treasure. Make your own pirate flags out of white sheet material and sticks, and set around the party room, hang on the wall, or place in the sand.

WHERE IN THE WORLD...

You can invite the whole world into your home—and make it the perfect place for your bon voyage party.

MATERIALS

* Paper or model airplanes, model train, plastic boats
* Flags from other countries
* Maps and globes of the world
* Travel posters, brochures, postcards
* Knickknacks, clothing, food from other countries
* Poster board
* Felt-tip pens

WHAT TO DO

Set up the departure area by decorating with pictures or miniatures of planes, trains, and boats. Hang model airplanes from the ceiling, set up a model train, and place boats in a tub of water as a table centerpiece. Put up international flags around the party room or hang them on the walls. (Make your own out of paper if you can't find a set of inexpensive ones.) Place maps on the walls or use a few to make a tablecloth. Set out an atlas and globe. Hang up travel posters, use postcards as place markers, and set out brochures. Gather together knickknacks, articles of clothing, or food from other countries. (Books about travel, transportation, and other countries are available at the library to offer ideas and inspiration.) Use poster board to make up travel signs such as "Bangkok," airport signs such as "Gate 9," common phrases in foreign languages such as "Bienvenue" or "Ou est le W.C.?" and hang them on the walls. Get out suitcases, set up chairs to form the interior of an airplane, train, bus, or cruise ship, and wear an outfit from another country during the party.

OTHER DECORATING TIPS

Here are some quickie tips to give your party room a boost!

* Cut out STARS from poster board and write the guest's names on them. Hang them from the ceiling or tape them to the walls. Make the birthday child's star larger and place it in the middle of the others.
* Take POLAROID PICTURES of the kids as they arrive at the party and glue each photo to a large sheet of construction paper. Cover with clear Con-Tact paper and use as place mats, then let them take the personalized place mats home.

* Make your party room ROYAL with a red carpet, crowns for the kings and queens, and posters of the royal family.
* Make FOOTPRINTS leading from the sidewalk to the party room, to let your guests know where to go.
* For a BIG & LITTLE party, get or make items extra-large or mini-sized and place them around the room. Try this idea with cookies or stars cut from construction paper.
* Make a giant TOY HOUSE by joining two large appliance boxes together. Paint the house with details on the inside and out, give it curtains and a carpet, and hold the party inside the "house."
* Decorate with BABY PICTURES of your guests, famous movie stars, or even pets.
* Create a SUNNY DAY when it's raining or snowing by painting a rainbow or a large happy sun bursting with rays on butcher

paper and hanging it on the wall. Make puffy clouds from polyester fiberfill and hang from the ceiling. Cut out pictures of birds or make your own from construction paper, and hang them from the ceiling. Play "Zippety-Doo-Dah" in the background.

* Place CARTOON CHARACTERS all over the party room, cut out of the Sunday funnies, comic books, coloring books, or inexpensive picture books.

* Clown around in the party room with CLOWNS. Make clown faces from construction paper and balloons, and dress them in funny clothing. Hang circus posters around the room.

* "Plant" FLOWERS all over the party room and turn it into a garden party. Make tissue paper flowers, buy artificial or real flowers, or cut them out of construction paper. Hang flower seed packets from the ceiling or use them as place markers. Scent the room with flowered air freshener, and give each guest a flower corsage.

* Create a HAWAIIAN ISLAND atmosphere with grass skirts, Hawaiian shirts, flower or candy leis, construction-paper palm trees, and Hawaiian music in the background.

* HANG UP funny or theme-related items from the ceiling. Hang up snacks, candies, cookies, musical notes, stars and planets, space ships and airplanes, toothbrushes, your guest's shoes, wrapped packages, or just about anything!

* Create a giant ZODIAC for your party room and write up large horoscopes for each of your guests. Make up funny ones to entertain the crowd—keep them optimistic!

* Rip out pages from MAGAZINES to fit the theme of your party. Place them on the walls, or use them as place mats and gift wrapping.

* MASKS AND COSTUMES make great decorations for your party. Set up dummies dressed in creative costumes to match the party theme, and place scary, ugly, and funny masks on the walls or party table. Use plain masks for invitations, place markers, and favors.

* Using white construction paper, make up a bunch of SPEECH BALLOONS and fill them

in with jokes, funny sayings, and comments about your guests. Tape them on the walls next to posters of movie stars or pictures of other guests, or use as place mats, where the guests have to figure out which speech balloon fits which party guest.

* Turn the party room into a SPORTSLAND and set up the party room with athletic equipment, posters of famous athletes, and other sports items. Make a centerpiece from sports injury items, such as Ben-Gay, Ace Bandages, and slings, for example.

* Create some UFOS, space ships, and outer-space creatures made from construction paper, Styrofoam, and other art materials. Hang them from the ceiling or along the walls, along with posters of your favorite TV space shows.

* Think about a COLOR SCHEME for your party if appropriate, such as orange and black during October, or red, white, and blue during July, for example.

GREAT
KID GAMES

The best part of a birthday party are the games and activities. After all, they are what make the party lively and fun! As a party planner, you'll need to provide lots of games to play during the celebration.

Pick party games that are designed for the children's ages and developmental levels; they should be challenging, yet not frustrating. Use the following game suggestions for the party, adapting to suit the theme, the location, the children's abilities, the amount of time you have, and the number of guests invited.

After each game, have plenty of inexpensive prizes on hand for the winners—and the losers! Keep a few extras for ties, unhappy children, or broken toys. That way everyone goes home with a small gift and a big smile.

If you have trouble involving one or two children in the games, ask a helper at the party to attend to those who are hesitant to participate. Encourage, but don't force anyone to play if they don't want to. Give the reluctant child something else to do, such as help out with the games, prepare for the next activity, or award the prizes.

Try to offer a quiet game to begin, perhaps one that helps the kids become acquainted if they don't know each other. Then play a couple of games that will use up some of their youthful energy—outside if possible—so the kids will have lots of room to run around, yell and scream, and avoid breaking things of value. End with a quiet game or activity to relax the kids and calm them down in preparation for opening the gifts and serving cake and ice cream. And always have more games and activities than you think you need, or you may end up with time on your hands and kids out of control.

Instead of games and activities, you may want to go on an outing that provides amusement for the kids, such as a visit to the zoo, ball park, skating rink, or science museum. Or ask a special talented guest to come and entertain the kids, such as a storyteller, clown, magician, or police officer.

Once you've got your games and activities planned, get on your mark, get set, go!

A-B-C GAME

All you have to know is the alphabet to play this hilarious and personalized game.

MATERIALS

* Alphabet chart, if desired

WHAT TO DO

Gather the players together in a circle. To begin the game, have the birthday child choose a letter. Have the player next to him or her say a sentence about the birthday child beginning with that letter. For example, if the birthday child chooses the letter "I," the first player could say something like "I'm glad it's your birthday," or "Isn't it great to have a birthday party?" The next player must say a sentence about the birthday child beginning with the next letter of the alphabet, in this example, "J." He or she might say, "Just wait until you open my present." The game continues around the circle, including the birthday person when it's his or her turn, until the entire alphabet has been used. So if you started with the letter "I," you'll end with the letter "H." When a round of play is over, choose another guest to honor or subject to discuss. Start with a different letter, and play the game again. The silly sentences sure to be thought up provide good laughs.

BALLOON BODYBUILDER

Pump up with this goofy game that will turn the kids into misshapen musclemen. The faster the play, the more the fun—and surprises—in store!

MATERIALS

* Dozens of small balloons
* 2 pairs of adult sweatsuits

WHAT TO DO

Divide the group into two teams and select one person from each team to be the Balloon Bodybuilder. Have them put the sweatsuits on

over their clothes. Distribute equal numbers of balloons to each group. Have the balloons already blown up for younger kids; let the older kids blow up their own as they play. On the word "Go!" the two teams must (blow up and) stuff as many balloons as they can into the sweatsuits of the Balloon Bodybuilders, trying not to pop the balloons as they go. Call time at three minutes and let the Balloon Bodybuilders show off their new physiques for a good laugh. Then have each team count the number of balloons that were stuffed as they remove them from under the bodybuilders' sweatsuits. Whoever used the most balloons, wins. Be sure to have a camera on hand for this one.

BLACK-OUT

Odd how everyday items when slightly altered can suddenly look like objects from outer space. See if the kids can tell what's what.

MATERIALS

* Everyday items from around the house, such as an eraser, a lens from sunglasses, a bottle top, a can of soup, a candy bar, a toothpaste cap, a cracker, a box of bandages, a computer disk, a compass, a video game box, a cookie, a ruler, a game die, a game board, a dog biscuit, a wad of foil
* Black spray paint

WHAT TO DO

Spray paint all the items black and allow to dry. Set them on a table. (Use a paper tablecloth and draw question marks all over it for fun.) Have the kids guess what the items are and write down their answers on a sheet of paper. When all the items have been guessed, reveal the answers and see who got the most right.

Or leave the items as is and place them in individual boxes. Have the guests feel the items without looking at them. Then have them guess what they are touching.

BODY BINGO

What do you get when you introduce Twister to Bingo? You get Body Bingo!

MATERIALS

* Large sheet of plastic (such as a shower curtain), bed sheet, or a large sheet of cardboard
* Acrylic paint or permanent felt-tip pens
* Index cards

WHAT TO DO

Spread out the plastic, cloth, or cardboard sheet and divide it into a grid, five squares across and five down, to make twenty-five squares. Outline the squares in black paint or felt-tip pen. Inside the squares, write names of the guests, or draw cartoons, pictures, or symbols. Or paint on traditional Bingo numbers and write the word "B-I-N-G-O" across the top. Write corresponding names, pictures, or numbers on the index cards. Place the cards in a hat or box. Have one player be the Master of Ceremonies and pull a card out of the box without looking, then read the card aloud. Another player must place a part of his or her body on the corresponding square on the grid. Continue until everyone has had a turn. Then begin again, continuing to pull out cards and having the players place other parts of their bodies on the grid. If a player loses his or her balance and falls, he or she is out of the game. The play continues until someone gets a Bingo, or there is only one remaining player.

BOMB SQUAD

The suspense may kill them as they race the clock to find the hidden—and still ticking—"bomb."

MATERIALS

* Alarm clock with a ticking sound

WHAT TO DO

Have the players leave the room. Wind up the clock and set it for three minutes. Hide it well in the party room, out of sight, but make sure the ticking sound is still audible. Have the players return to the room and tell them to listen for the "bomb." Tell them it's their job to find the bomb before it goes off in three minutes. If they listen carefully as they walk around the room, they'll detect the ticking sound. The suspense builds as the bomb squad tries to locate the clock before the alarm goes off. After a few successful searches, make it more challenging by setting the clock for two minutes, then one minute.

BOOGIE MAN

The Boogie Man will get you if you don't watch out!

MATERIALS

* Blindfolds for all players

WHAT TO DO

Gather the kids in a safe play area, such as a room with furniture removed or a grassy, fenced-in lawn. Choose one person to be the Boogie Man. Everyone puts on a blindfold, including the Boogie Man. When everyone is blindfolded—and very quiet—the Boogie Man tries to tag another player. The suspense is tremendous as the players slowly move around the room trying not to get tagged—but never

knowing exactly where the Boogie Man is. When the Boogie Man finally tags someone, that person becomes the Boogie Man.

Try this game in the swimming pool too, where everything moves in slow motion and the water masks the auditory clues.

BROKEN MIRROR

Things are not as they appear when you look into a Broken Mirror.

MATERIALS

* Silly accessories, such as hats, wigs, gloves, shoes, socks, capes, jewelry

WHAT TO DO

Give each player an accessory to wear and have them put the item on. Choose one player to leave the room. While he or she is out of sight, have the rest of the players exchange their accessories, so that everyone is wearing some-

thing else. Have the chosen player return to the room and figure out who was originally wearing what accessory. Give everyone a chance to leave the room and guess the changes.

To make it even more difficult, have the kids trade articles of their own clothing, or simply make an adjustment to their clothes while the chosen player is out of the room. For example, one player could take off his socks, another could put her watch on her other wrist, another could roll up his sleeves, while another could tie up her hair. Then have the chosen player guess what's different.

BUMBLING BUBBLE GUM

How hard can it be to open a piece of bubble gum? Not easy, when you're all fat thumbs.

MATERIALS

* Pair of large garden gloves or socks for each player
* Square piece of individually wrapped bubble gum for each player

WHAT TO DO

Give each child a pair of gloves, the bigger and floppier the better. Divide the players into two teams and line them up. Set the unopened bubble gum on a table next to the leaders of each team. At the signal, have the leaders take a piece of bubble gum, open it while wearing the gloves, and put the gum in their mouths. As soon as they're finished, they must take another piece of gum from the table and pass it to the next player, who must unwrap the gum and put it in his or her mouth. Repeat, passing the gum down the row, until the last person in line puts the last piece of gum in his or her mouth to win the game for that team. Try this game having the kids wear socks on their hands instead of gloves to make it a little more difficult. Then try it with your eyes closed!

CANDY GRAB

This game is a lot like the old favorite, "Spoons," but our version is much more fun!

MATERIALS

* Small individually wrapped candies or small toys
* Deck of cards

WHAT TO DO

Gather the guests in a circle, either on the floor or around a table. In the center of the floor or table, set out one fewer toy or piece of candy than there are players. Shuffle the cards and deal four to each player. Set the remaining cards next to the leader of the group. The leader draws a card, checks to see if he or she needs it to make a suit of four, then passes it or a card from his or her hand to the player on the left. This continues as cards are passed from player to player, with the leader moving rapidly to keep the game active. When a player finally collects four cards of the same suit, he very quietly steals a piece of candy or a toy from the center. When the other players notice a candy is missing, they must quickly grab one of the remaining candies, until all the candies are gone. At that point the last player will realize there are no more candies and has lost. The winners can keep their treats. Set up more candies or toys in the center of the table or floor again, and pass the cards.

CANDY WRAP

What could be easier than opening up a candy bar? Well, try it with the suggested utensils and see what happens!

MATERIALS

* Candy bar for each child (all the same kind or a variety)
* Dull knife and fork for each child
* Pair of chopsticks for each child

WHAT TO DO

Set out the wrapped candy bars on the table. Pass out the dull knives and forks to everyone. On the word "Go!" have them race to open the candy bars using only the knives and forks—no hands! The first to open a candy bar wins and gets an extra candy bar, while the others get to eat their own. When finished, try the game again with chopsticks. Or try again with a variety of hand-held tools, such as bacon tongs, wooden ice cream sticks, or spoons.

COCOON

Turn the little caterpillars into cocoons with this exciting wrap-up game!

MATERIALS

* Toilet paper rolls, colors preferred

WHAT TO DO

Divide the group into two teams and have each team choose one player to be the caterpillar/cocoon. Give the rest of the team players several rolls of toilet paper and tell them to wrap up the caterpillar—upright—from head to toe, except for the face. The team that creates a completed cocoon first wins the game. The fun comes when the kids try to wrap the caterpillar too fast and the toilet paper starts breaking. There are a lot of loose ends to tie up before this game is over.

COMMERCIAL CRAZY

You will be surprised at how many commercials the kids know by heart! Put that knowledge to good use with a game of Commercial Crazy.

MATERIALS

* Magazine ads for products
* Construction paper
* Tape recorder
* Packages from products that kids are familiar with, such as a cereal box, cracker box, peanut butter jar, jelly jar, soda can, juice concentrate can, chocolate syrup bottle, maple syrup bottle, aspirin bottle, spice bottle, soup can, stewed tomato can, spaghetti noodle box, lasagna noodle box, oatmeal box, Parmesan cheese can, boxed candies, boxed mints
* Spray paint, wrapping paper, or foil
* Black felt-tip pen
* Paper and pencil

WHAT TO DO

Cut out magazine advertisements for products, and mount them on construction paper. Cover or black out the product names. Hold up the pictures one at a time and let the players write down or call out their answers. Or tape record jingles from the TV and play the tape back at the party. Have the players guess what product is being advertised and jot down the answers or have a race to call them out.

Or collect as many packages as you can before the party, perhaps borrowing from neighbors and friends. Try to find some that are similar but not identical, yet represent a particular kind of food. Spray paint all the containers or wrap them in wrapping paper or foil. Set the items on a table and write obscure clues on each container with black felt-tip pen. You might write "white-out" on the toothpaste box, "can you catch up?" on the tomato can, or just jot down some of the ingredients from the product, such as "contains fat, cholesterol, and sugar" on the candy box. Gather the players around the table and show each item. Have the kids write down what they think each item is. Award a prize to the player who can identify the most items correctly. You can make the game harder by not offering any clues. Or have a lot of products that are very similar in size and shape to make it even more challenging.

Or wrap all different kinds of candy bars in foil as tightly as you can and have the kids guess the candy by its shape. As each player guesses a candy bar, let them keep it and drop out of the game.

CRIME SCENE

You set the scene and let the young detectives solve the crime.

MATERIALS

* Items to use as clues, such as an obituary page from the newspaper, lipstick, a notepad with a time written on the top sheet, a broken pencil, a pair of eyeglasses, a few human hairs, a key, a check stub, a book of matches from a restaurant, a book with a page marked and a word circled inside, a fingerprint on a piece of paper, a sentence written in code, a piece of string or fabric
* Paper and pencil

WHAT TO DO

You can play this game in a couple of ways. If you want to plan the crime ahead of time, think up a scenario using the above items or those of your choosing. Arrange the clues on a table for the detectives to examine and see who comes up with a solution for the following questions:

Whodunit?

Who was the victim?

What was the weapon?

What was the motive?

When did it happen?

Where did it happen?

What exactly happened?

Be sure you have prepared answers for the above questions and have provided clues for all of them.

Or simply set out a bunch of clues, such as the ones above, and divide the group into several teams. Have them examine the scene of the crime, take notes, and possibly shoot a Polaroid picture of the clues. Then have each team meet in a separate room to figure out a logical sequence of events based on the evidence. Have the teams read their solutions to the group.

DETECTIVE

How well do the kids really know one another? Let them play Detective and find out the truth behind those innocent faces.

MATERIALS

* Sheet of paper for each player
* Pencil for each player

WHAT TO DO

While the party is just beginning, step aside and write down observations about each of the kids on a sheet of paper, such as "untucked shirt," "broken glasses," "backwards baseball cap," "hightop shoes," "chewing gum," "spot of catsup," "knotted shoelace," "open fly," and so on. Recopy the paper or print it out on the computer for each player and hand out the sheets. Have the players try to guess the kids who are described on the paper by writing in names beside the descriptions. The first one to guess them all correctly is the winner.

Or call the parents of the guests before the party, ask some questions about their past, such as "What was your child's nickname?", "Where was your child born?", "What's your child's favorite food?", and so on. Write the answers down on cards and read them aloud during game time. See who can guess which guests belong to which answers on the cards.

DICTIONARY

From the moment they learn to talk, kids love to play with words. Here's a game that will expand their vocabulary while providing lots of laughs.

MATERIALS

* Dictionary
* Paper and pencil for each player
* Timer

WHAT TO DO

Have the players sit at the table with pencil, paper, and a dictionary. The first player flips through the dictionary, chooses an unfamiliar word, and announces it to the group. It might be a word like "epizootic," which translates to "animal disease," "fug," which means "bad spell," "dowsabel," a word you'd use for your "sweetheart," "foozle," a "bad golf stroke," or "chuffy," which means "fat." After the first player announces the word, the rest of the players write down made-up definitions for the word. In the meantime, the first player writes down a paraphrase of the real definition. The first player then collects all the definitions, mixes them up, then reads them to the group. All the players must try to guess which definition is the real one. Each player gets a point for guessing the right definition, and a point for fooling one of the other players into choosing his or her made-up definition.

DO-IT DICE

This game is so easy, all you have to do is roll the dice and just Do It! Actually, it's not THAT easy . . .

MATERIALS

* 2 large cardboard boxes, approximately 1-foot square (available at the mailing and package stores)
* White spray paint or solid colored wrapping paper
* Permanent felt-tip pens

WHAT TO DO

Prepare the boxes by spray painting them white or by covering them with solid colored wrapping paper, and decorate to create a pair of large dice. On the outside of one die, write challenges, such as "Whistle a Tune," "Rub Your Head," "Clap Your Hands," "Turn Around," "Snap Your Fingers," and "Quack Like a Duck." On the other die, write more challenges, such as "Walk Backwards," "Flap Your Arms," "Touch Your Toes," "Sing a Song,"

"Bend Your Knees," and "Shake Your Head." Have a player roll the big dice, one die at a time. The player must meet the challenge written on both of the dice at the same time! For example, he might roll "Rub Your Head" and "Walk Backwards." If the player cannot do both challenges at the same time, he or she is out of the game. To make it even more challenging, add a third die with more challenges. You might want to make the challenges coordinate with the party theme.

FOLLOW THE FOOTPRINTS

Here's a game that can be adapted for lots of party themes. Try this as a starting point.

MATERIALS

* Construction paper
* Felt-tip pens

WHAT TO DO

Cut out a series of footprints from construction paper following a shoe pattern, or make animal footprints or big bare feet. Place the footprints in a twisty path from one end of the play area to the other. Make an identical path a few feet away from the first path. Divide the kids into two teams and have them race against each other along each footprint path. Remind them to keep their feet on the footprints for the whole race. To make it more challenging, make the footprints walk around, over, through, and under different objects, or make them twist around from front to back and sideways for part of the path. Make the footprints different colors and have the kids do a Mother-May-I race, stepping only on the colors that are announced.

FUNNY FASHION SHOW RELAY

This is the strangest, funniest fashion show you'll ever see, so keep the camera handy!

MATERIALS

* 2 suitcases
* 2 sets of clothing, including
  pants, shirt, jacket, hat, gloves,
  socks, shoes, jewelry, tie, wig
  (the funnier-looking the better)

* 2 sets of makeup, including
  lipstick, eye liner, and blush
  (optional)

WHAT TO DO

Fill the two suitcases with a complete set of
clothing and makeup. Divide the group into two
teams and give each team a filled suitcase. At
the signal, the first players on each team must
put on all the clothes over their own clothes
and the makeup—without a mirror—as quickly
as possible. When they're fully dressed, they
must take off all the clothes, put them back in
the suitcases with the makeup, and pass them
to the next players in line. This continues down
the line until one team finishes the dressing and
undressing before the other team. You can pack
the suitcases to suit the theme of your party, by
including nightwear for a slumber party, sixties
styles for a hippie party, or animal costumes for
a zoo party. If you have a swimming pool, it's
fun to play this in the water!

GIANT'S GAME

Enough of the small stuff! It's time to play a life-
sized Giant's Game where the party room
becomes the game board and playing pieces
are the kids.

MATERIALS

* A favorite board game that progresses from
  a starting point to a finish line, such as
  Candyland, Chutes and Ladders, Life,
  Careers, or Chinese Checkers
* Several packages of construction paper
* 2 square boxes
* White spray paint
* Large permanent black felt-tip pen

WHAT TO DO

Using a favorite board game as a model, plan the layout of the game to take place in the party room. Make the game squares out of colored construction paper, and number or label them the way they are in the game. Include details from the board game, making them life-sized too. Spray paint two large square boxes with white paint, and decorate them to look like giant dice. Then play the Giant's Game according to the rules from the board game. The kids are the playing pieces and they must move from square to square until someone reaches the finish line.

GIGGLE-GUT

No matter how hard you try, you won't be able to keep yourself from laughing at this tummy-tickling game.

MATERIALS

* None

WHAT TO DO

You'll need a large space to play this game, either inside or outside. Gather the kids in a circle and have them lie down on the floor, with one child placing his or her head on another child's tummy. The circle should connect with everyone lying on another player's tummy. Begin with the birthday child, who must say one simple word: "Ha!" Then have the second player—the one who's head is resting on the birthday child's tummy—say two words: "Ha! Ha!" Repeat for the next player and the next, adding more and more "Ha!"s until suddenly the giggles break out uncontrollably, everyone is laughing, and all the heads are bobbing up and down from the movement of the tummy-pillows. Try it a second time, reversing heads and tummies. Or have them say or make up silly words instead of "Ha!" such as "Magillacuddy!" or "Biggle-Boggle!" Have the players try not to break into laughter to see if they can make it all the way around without giggling. Bet it can't be done!

GO FISHING

This is a hands-on, get-wet, try-your-luck game that will entertain the kids at a number of different parties.

MATERIALS

* Plastic wading pool
* Floatable, wind-up plastic toys
* Small fishing nets

WHAT TO DO

Fill the wading pool with water and add small floatable plastic water toys that you wind up or that come with batteries—the kind that "swim" in the water. Have the kids try to catch the toys, one at a time, with their hands or with little fishing nets. For a bigger challenge, have them try to catch the toys with their eyes closed!

GOOFY FACE

The straight faces won't last long after a few minutes when playing Goofy Face. And no special materials are required—except a goofy face—and kids have plenty of those.

MATERIALS

* None

Have the kids sit in a line on the floor. The first player in line begins by creating a goofy face. He or she must "pass" that goofy face onto the next player in line, who then makes that same face, turns to the next player, and repeats the goofy face. Continue down the line until the last player receives the goofy face. Have the last player and the first player make the goofy faces at the same time and see if they came out the same. Repeat, having the first player go to the end of the line and the second player creating a new goofy face. You can play this with goofy movements using different parts of the body, goofy poses using your whole body, or with goofy drawings on pads of paper.

GOOSE FEATHERS

What could be more fun than an exciting game of chasing tail feathers? Go get 'em, Goose.

MATERIALS

* Large quill-type feather for each player

Have the geese sit in a circle, and tuck a large feather into the back of their pants or shirts. Choose a player to be the Fox, who is hungry and wants his goose dinner. The Fox walks around the outside of the circle as the geese sit quietly waiting for him to attack. Suddenly the Fox grabs a tail feather from the back of one player and runs as quickly as he can around the circle to the spot where the goose once sat. In the meantime the goose must leap up quickly to chase the Fox and try to catch him. If he catches the Fox, he is saved and can go back to the goose circle. If the Fox beats him to his spot, the goose becomes the Fox and it's his turn to search for a goose dinner and pull out a tail feather. If you prefer, use scraps of cloth hanging down the backs of the players instead of feathers, or substitute hats, scarves, sticky notes, loose shoes, or small toys.

HEART SURGEON

Oh dear! The kids are missing their hearts and they have to be replaced. It's time for the Heart Surgeon to operate!

MATERIALS

* Long sheet of butcher paper for each player
* Felt-tip pens, crayons
* Red construction paper
* Double-stick tape

WHAT TO DO

Lay out the butcher paper on the floor and let the kids trace one another's body outline on the paper. After they have made the outlines, have them draw in their faces, clothing, and other details. Using crayons or felt-tip pens, have the kids dress up their pictures in costumes and become Superheroes, Royalty, Rock Stars, Nerds, or Bathing Beauties. Have the kids draw in where their missing hearts should go, by outlining a heart in red felt-tip pen or crayon. Hang the pictures on a wall. Give each child a red heart cut from construction paper with double stick tape on the back. Have them close their eyes, or blindfold them, and let them try to place the heart in the heart outline. Whoever gets closest is the best surgeon and wins a prize. Play with other body parts if you like, such as the liver, the tongue, the guts, or the bellybutton.

HOPPIN' HATS

Be prepared for screams, laughs, and lots of excitement when you play Hoppin' Hats. It's probably best to play outside, where the kids can really cut loose.

MATERIALS

* 2 paper or plastic bowls per player
* Glue
* 1/4-inch elastic, approximately 4 inches for each player
* Small balls such as tennis balls, Koosh balls, Ping-Pong balls, rubber balls, or small bean bags

WHAT TO DO

Before the party begins, glue the bottoms of two bowls together (one set per player) and allow to dry. Punch two holes in each side of one bowl and attach elastic to make a chin strap. Let the kids decorate the hat/bowls as an activity or decorate them yourself ahead of time. Have the kids pair up and stand opposite each other, several feet apart, with the hat/bowls on their heads. Have one player try to toss a ball into the other player's hat/bowl. For a variation, have each player try to toss the ball or beanbag into their own hat/bowl. Keep the camera handy!

HOT LAVA

This game looks easy but it becomes more and more difficult to keep from falling into the Hot Lava.

MATERIALS

* Wood plank, approximately 6 inches wide by 8 feet long or an 8-foot-long rope
* 2 bricks or blocks to support the plank
* Swimming pool, kiddy pool, wet lawn, ice cubes or other substance to step in when you fall off the plank

WHAT TO DO

Set a plank over the shallow end of a swimming pool, across a kiddy pool, on a wet lawn, or set ice cubes along each side of the plank. (If you don't have a piece of wood, you can use a rope and simply place it on a wet lawn.) Have the kids walk the plank over the "hot lava" in a variety of ways, increasing in difficulty, until you have only one player left who hasn't "fallen" off the plank. Begin with a straight walk over the plank, then walk sideways, then backwards. Next have two players start from either end and attempt to cross paths to reach the opposite ends. Finally, have them walk with their eyes closed, which is nearly impossible! When they fall into the "hot lava," have them sit out the rest of the game while watching others meet the same fate.

MAGAZINE SCAVENGER HUNT

Have a Scavenger Hunt using magazines. Players won't even have to leave the party room!

MATERIALS

* Magazines with lots of pictures
* Sheets of paper
* Pen or pencil

WHAT TO DO

Before the party begins, write down a number of items the kids are likely to find in the magazines you have selected. Make enough copies of the list for several small teams. At game time, divide the players into teams of three or four. Give each team a magazine and a list of items to find inside the magazines. Have the kids search through the magazines and rip out the items on the list until they have every one, or time is called. The first to finish—or get the most items—wins.

MIND READER

Don't you often wish you could read people's minds? In this game, it seems like you can!

MATERIALS

* Paper and pencil
* Prewritten questions

WHAT TO DO

Prepare for the game by writing questions for the players ahead of time. The questions should be unpredictable, but easy to answer and fun. For example, "What did you have for break-fast?", "Who's your favorite cartoon character?", "What month is your birthday?", "What do you want to be when you grow up?", "What is your favorite vacation spot?", "When do you plan to get married?", or "When did you learn to ride a bike?" To begin, have the guests sit in a circle and give them each paper and a pencil. Place the prewritten questions in a hat or bowl and have each player pick a question. Each player must write down an answer to the question received, then returns the question to the bowl. The answers are kept by the players. When all have finished, pass the bowl to one player. That player draws a question and reads it aloud. The player who originally got that question raises his or her hand. Now the player who has just drawn the question must try to guess the answer written by the original player to win a prize.

MORTUARY

Sounds spooky but it's a lot of fun. And even more so in the dark. . . .

MATERIALS

* Fruits and vegetables to simulate body parts: 2 peeled grapes (for eyes), canned peach half (for tongue), dozen popcorn kernels (for teeth), cooked spaghetti (for brain), cooked rigatoni (for intestines), slab of firm Jell-O (for liver), peeled tomato (for heart), limp, wilted carrot stick (for finger)
* Small paper bags lined with plastic bags
* Felt-tip pen
* Paper and pencil

WHAT TO DO

Prepare the food items above and place them in individual paper bags lined with plastic bags. Number each bag with a felt-tip pen. Pass out paper and pencil. Sitting in a circle in a semi-dark room, make up a story about the autopsy of a dead body, or other horror story involving body parts—but don't make it too scary! As you mention each body part, pass around a bag with the corresponding "body part" inside. Tell the kids to feel inside the bag and write down what they think it really is (or have them just say it out loud after everyone has had a turn). Show them everything at the end of the guessing game.

NAME THE TUNE

Can they name the tune in three notes? How many notes will it take for the kids to recognize their favorite tunes? Play Name the Tune and find out.

MATERIALS

* Radio or
* CDs, tapes, or albums
* Tape recorder and cassette

WHAT TO DO

Have the kids sit in a circle around the radio. Turn the radio dial slowly. When you come to a station that is playing a song, have the players quickly try to guess the name of the song before the rest of the guests. Award a point for the right title. You might also have them name the singer or group for another point, the year for another point, the type of music for another point, and so on. If you prefer, record a few bars of a number of songs before the party begins, and play the tape during the game. Allow some time between songs for the players to guess the name of the song.

ODDBALL OLYMPICS

Turn the party into the Oddball Olympics with lots of slightly strange competitions and challenges.

MATERIALS

* 2 identical boxes and small toys or candies to put inside the boxes
* Tennis balls, rubber balls, plastic balls, Whiffle balls, Koosh balls
* Ping-Pong paddle for each player and balloons
* 12 empty soda cans and a tennis or plastic ball

* Baseball mitt, garden glove, plastic bucket, baseball cap, small box, cloth bag, butterfly net or anything else to catch with for each player and 1 ball
* Empty cans, golf balls, and a yardstick or broom handle for each player
* Wooden planks, chairs, ropes

WHAT TO DO

BALANCE BEAN

Collect two identical small boxes that the kids can balance on their heads. Line up two teams and place a box on the heads of the first players of each team. Have another team member place a toy or candy in the box, then tell the first player to walk to the other side of a set path and back without dropping the box or the item inside. If the player finishes without dropping the box with the toy or candy inside, he or she passes the box to the next player and another item is put into the box. If a player drops the box, he must start over. Continue until every member of a team makes it all the way through without dropping the box of toys or candies.

BALL BLITZ

Line up two teams and set a pile of balls at both ends of the play area. In addition to the balls listed above, you might include a golf ball, marble, Ping-Pong ball, Super ball, or jaw-breaker. Have the first players on each team take a ball from the pile, run to the opposite side, pick up a ball and run back, then hand off the two balls to the second player who must also pick up another ball, run to the other side, get another ball, and run back. The game continues until someone drops a ball, or a team finishes collecting all the balls first.

BALLOON BADMINTON

Have the kids stand in a large circle, each one holding one Ping-Pong paddle. Have the first player hit a balloon to the next player using his paddle. The next player must hit the balloon to the next person in the circle, also using his paddle. If a player misses, he or she is out of the game until only one player remains.

BOWLING BATTLE

Set out the empty soda cans in a bowling pin formation. Have the players stand back a good distance and roll a tennis ball or plastic ball to the cans, in an effort to knock them over. Keep score or just see who knocks over the most cans. Let the kids be creative in how they set up the cans.

CRAZY CATCH

Have the players stand in a circle, and give each one an object for catching a ball, such as a mitt, glove, bucket, or cap. Have one player toss the ball across the circle to another player, who must catch the ball with the item he or she is holding. If a player misses, he or she is out of the game. Repeat the game over and over, rotating the catching items so the kids can have a chance to use them all.

GOOFY GOLF

Set out empty cans tipped on their sides to be the golf holes. Give each player a yardstick or broom handle to use as a golf club. Create a path from one can to another, and let the kids hit golf balls, Ping-Pong balls, or tennis balls along the golf course. Add a few sand and water traps with bowls and pans, and set up other obstacles as well.

OBNOXIOUS OBSTACLES

Set up the yard in an obstacle course, with planks to walk on, chairs to crawl under, ropes to jump over, and winding paths to follow. Have each player try to get through the obstacle course in record time, by timing him with a stop watch. Then have the players try the course blindfolded, with their hands tied behind their backs, or backwards.

PASS THE PRESENT

Everyone gets a gift in Pass the Present—but which gift? That's the question!

MATERIALS

* A small toy, candy, or gift for each player, with some booby prizes, such as giant underwear or a box of prunes
* Small boxes or bags to hold gifts
* Wrapping paper
* Index cards
* Felt-tip pens

WHAT TO DO

Buy a small inexpensive item for each child or have each guest bring a small gift for another child. Wrap them up individually in fancy boxes or bags, or wrap them in lots of crazy ways to make them unique and intriguing. Write numbers on the index cards, one for each player. Have the player who picks number one choose a wrapped gift and open it. Have the next player choose from the remaining gifts, and so on, until all the gifts have been opened. For variation, give the second player the option of choosing a wrapped gift or taking away the gift from player number one.

Or write numbers on the bottoms of the gifts and pass them to all the players sitting in a circle. Play music, then stop the music and have the player who has gift number one open it and drop out of the circle; repeat.

PICTURE PUZZLE

A Picture Puzzle isn't an ordinary puzzle the kids put together. This one packs a surprise when it's finished.

MATERIALS

* A 5 by 7-inch or 8½ by 11-inch photo of each player
* Tagboard
* Spray adhesive
* Large manila envelope for each player

WHAT TO DO

Gather photos of all the guests from their parents (and promise to return them!). Take the pictures to the photocopy store and reproduce them. Enlarge the photocopy to a standard size if the photo is too small. Spray adhesive on a sheet of tagboard cut to the size of the picture and allow to dry. Repeat for all the pictures. Cut each picture into puzzle shapes and drop the pieces into its own large manila envelope. Mark which picture is inside using your own code. Give each guest an envelope with his secretly marked picture inside, and at the signal, have them all race to see who can finish their puzzles first. Watch the surprised faces as they realize who is being put back together! To make it harder, mix up all the pieces in a pile and have the kids race to complete a puzzle first.

POISON!

Watch out! All those tasty-looking goodies are tempting. But one of them is POISON!

MATERIALS

* A variety of small candies, nuts, dried fruit, crackers, cereals, or other treats, one of each per player
* A large platter

WHAT TO DO

Set out one of each treat for each player on a platter. Have one player leave the room. While that player is gone, select one of the treats to be "poison." Have the player return to the room and choose a small treat to eat. If he eats a treat that is not poison, he takes another treat, proceeding through the platter items to the last one—the one that is poison—or until he bites into the poison treat and the groups yells out "Poison!" Select another player to leave the room and play again.

For a variation on this game, have everyone close their eyes while one child selects a treat to be "poison." Have the player mark the bottom of the treat using the decorator tip on a tube of frosting, then replace the item on the platter. Have the players open their eyes and one at a time select a treat to eat, without looking at the bottom of the treat to see if it's marked. If a player eats a poison treat, the one who marked it calls out "Poison!" and the player is out of the game. Continue until only one player is left.

PRIZE IS RIGHT

Much like the television show, *The Price Is Right,* but this game makes a winner out of everyone.

MATERIALS

* A collection of inexpensive fun items, such as candy bars, small toys, cards, comics, cassette singles, art materials
* Paper and pencil

WHAT TO DO

As you buy items for the game, keep track of the prices. Then write down the prices of each item on tags and to place underneath each item, face down on the table. Have each of the players try to guess the exact price of each item as you hold them up, one at a time. Ask them to write down an estimate of the price on a piece of paper. When everyone has written a guess, have the players hold up their answers. Announce the actual price of the featured item. Whoever guesses closest to the actual price wins that item as a prize and drops out of the game so the rest can have a chance to win something.

QUICKSAND

Here's a "refreshing" twist to an old favorite, Musical Chairs. But this version is played while wearing bathing suits!

MATERIALS

* Buckets, large bowls, pans, or other large water containers
* Portable radio or cassette player

WHAT TO DO

Set the bowls out on the lawn in a circle, one for every player. Fill one bowl with water and leave the rest empty. Play the radio or a musical cassette and have the players walk around the bowls as the music plays. When the music stops, everyone must sit down in a bowl. The player who is forced to sit in the water-filled bowl is out. Remove a bowl and continue playing until only one player remains.

For more water fun, play the traditional musical chairs and fill ALL the bowls or buckets with water. Set out one less bucket than there are players to begin the game, then start the music and have the kids march around the circle of water buckets. When the music stops, they must sit down in a water-filled bucket; the player who doesn't find a bucket to sit in is out. Continue until only one player is left—and everyone is wet!

SCREEN TEST

If the eyes look familiar but you can't place the nose, you're ready to be a contestant at our Screen Test.

MATERIALS

* Large pictures of famous people
  or characters

* Large manila envelopes
* Stickers
* Scissors

WHAT TO DO

Collect pictures of people, cartoon characters, monsters, puppets, and animals that will be familiar to the guests. Try to choose large pictures, 5 by 7-inches or 8 1/2 by 11-inches so they're easy to see. Cut three sides of a small square (about 1 inch by 1 inch) on the front of the envelope, leaving one side uncut to make a window flap. Repeat until you have ten "windows" scattered over the front of the envelope. Place a picture inside the envelope facing the front. Make sure all the windows are closed and seal them shut with stickers. Repeat for several envelopes. Gather the kids in a circle and hold up one envelope. Have one player select a window, remove the sticker, and open the window. That player must then guess who is featured in the picture. If he or she can't, the next player gets a turn to open a window and guess the picture. Continue until someone guesses the person or thing, or all the

windows are open. Play again with another envelope, starting with a different player.

SHOE LOOSE

Can the kids recognize their own shoes if put to the test? It's not an easy "feet" when they play the Shoe Loose game.

MATERIALS

* The players' shoes
* Blindfolds for all players

WHAT TO DO

Have the players sit in a circle and remove their shoes. Set one shoe aside and toss the other one into the middle of the circle in a pile. Blindfold all the players and mix up the shoes. At the signal, have the players scramble to the pile, locate their own shoe, and put it on. The player who gets his or her shoe on first, wins.

To make it more difficult, include both shoes in the pile and have the players put them both on. Or have the kids wear a certain style of shoe to the party, such as athletic shoes. You might also want to play the game one at a time, having each child in the circle take a turn with the blindfold to hunt for his or her shoes. This way the other players can watch the fun.

SNAP–OR ZAP!

Here's an updated version of the classic game, "Categories," which has been entertaining kids for years.

MATERIALS

* None

WHAT TO DO

Players sit in a circle cross-legged on the floor. The first player chooses a category, such as "Colors," "Boy's Names," "Candy Bars," "TV Shows," "Clothing," "Pizza Toppings," "Fast Food Restaurants," and so on. All players slap their thighs in unison, then clap their hands, then snap their fingers. When the leader snaps his or her fingers, he or she must call out one item from the category. If it's "Pizza Toppings," the leader might say "Cheese!" The next player must call out a different item from the category on the very next "snap!" without missing a beat. If that player can't come up with a "snap,"—"Zap!" he or she is out of the game. Play continues until there is only one person left. To make it more exciting, have each player point to another player instead of passing the turn around in a predictable circle. In this suspenseful version, no one knows exactly when they'll be called on next.

SOUND STAGE

Listen! Do you hear that sound? Sure you do! But can you identify it? Now that's the tricky part!

MATERIALS

* Cassette recorder and tape
* Paper and pencil

WHAT TO DO

Before the party begins, tape record a series of ten or twelve sounds you hear around the house and/or outside. For example, you might record a toilet flush, a garden hose being turned on, a toaster popping up, an alarm clock going off, keys being tapped on a computer, a phone ring or a busy signal, a doorbell ring, a coffee-maker perking, a pencil sharpener grinding, a tea kettle whistling, a car motor revving up, a car door slamming shut, a police siren, a jar being opened. Leave a few seconds of silence in between each sound. Play the cassette to the group and have them write down the sounds they hear. Whoever guesses the most number of sounds correctly wins a prize. For a variation, tape record the kids saying, "Happy Birthday" to the birthday child as they enter the party, then play back the tape and let them try to guess who's talking. Or record familiar voices from the TV and have the kids guess the celebrity's voice.

STEP 'N' POP

A high-energy game that will keep them hoppin' till they drop.

MATERIALS

* Balloons for each player
* String

WHAT TO DO

You'll need to go outside to play this game, preferably on concrete. Blow up balloons and tie one balloon to an ankle of each player. At the signal, have the players try to pop one another's balloons by stepping on them. If you prefer, divide the kids up into pairs and have them try to pop only their partner's balloon. Tie balloons to both ankles to make it even more challenging.

TAIL TAG

When the kids want to act like wild animals, take them outside and play Tail Tag!

MATERIALS

* Cloth tail, approximately 2 inches wide by 1 foot long, for each player
* Permanent felt-tip pens

WHAT TO DO

Make cloth tails from a variety of leftover fabric, so each one is different. Or use white sheeting cut into lengths and let the kids color their tails with permanent felt-tip pens. Fringe the ends by pulling threads if you want a donkey-style tail. Tie a knot at one end and have the players tuck the knotted end into the back of their pants, with the "tail" hanging free. Have the players line up on opposite sides of the play area. Have one group be the hunters, who don't wear tails, and the other group be the animals, who do wear tails. The hunter group must try to grab off an animal's tail while the animal tries to run to the other side for safety.

Or have one player, without a tail, stand on one side of the play area while the rest, with tails, stand on the other side. Have the ones with tails run one at a time across to the other side, trying to avoid having their tails snatched. If a player makes it to the other side, he or she is safe. If a player's tail is snatched, he or she must help the player without the tail catch the next player who tries to run across.

TASTER'S TONGUE

The taster's tongue creates some funny faces on the players, so get ready to snap some pictures.

MATERIALS

* A variety of foods in small bowls covered with foil
* Plastic spoons
* Paper and pencil

WHAT TO DO

Prepare a variety of foods in small bowls, such as honey, cereal, applesauce, oatmeal, mashed bananas, yogurt, scrambled eggs, mashed dev-iled egg, spaghetti sauce, macaroni and cheese, melted ice cream, milkshake, fruit salad, soup, pudding, and creamed corn. Cover the bowls with foil so the players can't see the contents, and give each bowl a number. Give the kids a spoon for each bowl of food (to prevent spreading germs). Have them close their eyes and pass around one bowl of food. As they taste the food, have them write down their guesses under the corresponding numbers. When all the foods have been passed around and tasted, remove the foil, reveal the contents, and see how many flavors they were able to identify. To make the game more challenging, choose foods that are very similar in taste or texture. For example, use all baby foods, all cereals, all sauces, all mashed fruit, or all soups.

THIEF!

Even your best friends may steal from you in this just-for-fun game!

MATERIALS

* 3 different small candy bars or toys for each player
* 2 decks of cards

WHAT TO DO

Have the kids sit in a circle on the floor or at the table. Place all the treats in the middle of the group. Pass out three cards from one deck to each player, face up in front of them. From the second deck, hold up a card, one at a time. If the card matches one of the player's cards, the first player gets to take a favorite treat from the center pile and place it out of sight so no one can see it. Continue playing until all the treats are gone and everyone has three each. Reshuffle the first deck, give each player one card, and have them keep it secret. Display a card from the second deck, one at a time, until a player has a match with the hidden card. The player who has a match then gets to "steal" a treat from another player, AFTER identifying the name of the item and who has it. If the player can name both, he or she gets to steal the treat, leaving the second player with only two treats and adding one to his or her own pile of three. If wrong, a treat is given to the player who was nearly robbed. Play until everyone has been a thief.

THINK FAST

Some games exercise the body, this game exercises the mind—and keeps it moving fast!

MATERIALS

* Medium-sized ball

WHAT TO DO

Gather all the players outside and have them form a circle. Toss the ball to one player and have him name a category, such as "animals," "candy bars," "cartoon characters," or "snacks," for example. When the game begins, the player with the ball must toss the ball to another player. As the second player catches the ball, he must name an item from the chosen category within three seconds. Then he must toss the ball to another player who must also name another item from the same category within three seconds. The game continues until someone is caught holding the ball too long or cannot come up with a new item in the category. Change categories and play again.

TREASURE HUNT

It's so much fun to find buried treasure, especially when the hunt is guided by a treasure map.

MATERIALS

* Cardboard box, old lunch box, or other container
* Gold spray paint
* Chocolate coins in gold foil, fake jewelry, small toys and candies
* Large sheet of white paper
* Felt-tip pens

WHAT TO DO

Spray paint a box with gold paint and allow to dry. Mark with pirate markings or other interesting signs or stickers. Fill with chocolate coins, fake jewelry, and small gifts for the kids. Hide or bury the treasure chest in the backyard, park, beach, or forest. Create a treasure map to lead the kids from the starting point to the buried treasure. You can make the map in several different ways. Give them pictures of landmarks to follow, or count out the paces and mark them with dotted lines; give clues to lead them from one point to another, or cut up the map and give them parts at a time, with one part leading to the discovery of another part. Just don't make it too easy or too hard. Then let them follow the clues to the buried treasure.

WATER BALLOON BLAST-OFF

A wet and wild game to play at the pool or beach party.

MATERIALS

* 2 plastic funnels
* 4 (8-foot) lengths of rubber surgical tubing (available at hardware supply and craft stores)
* Rope

WHAT TO DO

Before the party, make holes in both sides of the funnels with a sharp skewer or drill. Tie two pieces of rubber tubing to both sides of the funnels to create a giant slingshot.

At the party, separate the kids into two teams of three players. Set up the "goal" by tying a rope between two trees, or laying it on the ground in a straight line or a circle, depending on how you want the target. Fill up balloons with water. Have two players from one team hold each end of the rubber tubing, with the funnel in between them both. Have a third player place a water balloon in the funnel, standing several feet from the goal, and launch it toward the goal. Note the point where it lands, and whether or not it flew over the rope or into the circle, depending on what you have set up. Have the other team launch their water balloon, and see who got closest to the goal. Or have both teams play at the same time. Or launch them at one another's teams and see how many players they can get wet!

WATER BRIGADE

Watch the kids get wet with this wild water game!

MATERIALS

* 4 large buckets or pans of water
* Small plastic bowl, bucket, cup, or other water container for each player

WHAT TO DO

Break up the group into two teams and line them up outside in a play area. Place a large bucket at the end of each line. At the beginning of each line, set out enough bowls or cups for each player, and a large bucket of water. When you give the signal, have the first player fill a cup with water out of the bucket and pass it to the next player, who must pass it to the next, and so on, until it reaches the end of the line. At that point the last player must pour the water into the large empty bucket. As soon as the first player has passed the first cup of water to the second player, he must immediately get another cup, fill it with water, and pass it down the row, moving as quickly as possible while trying not to spill any water. This fast-moving game should get everyone a little wet, as they all make an effort to fill the last big bucket with water. You can award a prize to the team that

finished first, or a prize to the team that has the most water in the last bucket, or both.

Another method of passing the water is to have each player begin by holding an empty cup, and having the first player pour water into the second player's cup, then the second player pouring it into the third player's cup, and so on, down the line. In the meantime, the first player refills his cup and begins the pouring procession down the line once again. Repeat until the first bucket is empty of water. To make the game more challenging, have the players pass the cups or bowls of water over their heads to the next player. And for fun, use different shapes and sizes of containers for passing the water, such as measuring cups, plastic spoons, rimmed baking sheets, large bowls, muffin tins, and plastic baby bottles. Also try large sponges, water balloons, or turkey basters.

WINKER

Keep your eyes open for this subtle game if you want to be a Winker winner.

MATERIALS

* Deck of cards

WHAT TO DO

Have all the players sit around in a circle on the floor or at the table. Remove a card from the deck for each player, choosing all black cards except for one red. Mix up the cards and pass them face down to all the players. Start a conversation and tell the players to join in the discussion. For example, you can talk about your day, discuss a movie you've all seen, or tell what you had for breakfast. While people are talking, the person who was given the red card is the "Winker." He must wink at another player in the circle surreptitiously, without being caught by any of the other players—not an easy task. And he must do it within three minutes of play. After he winks at someone without getting caught, the player who was winked at should wait a few moments so it's not obvious who winked at him, then call out, "I'm dead!" He's out of the game temporarily, as the Winker continues to try to eventually wink at every player and "kill" them, without being caught by the other players. Each winked-at player must announce they are "dead" after a short delay. The game ends when the last player is "killed" or the Winker gets caught when a player catches him winking at another player.

AWESOME ACTIVITIES

As a nice balance to the excitement of the games, plan some quieter activities that are fun, creative, and unique to the party's theme. In the following pages, you'll find lots of suggestions for things to make and do that should keep hands busy and minds occupied for a good portion of the party.

In addition to arts, crafts, and other activities, you might want to hire a special guest to make an appearance at your child's party, someone who can provide a special activity, such as a magician or clown, a storyteller or actor, a recreation leader, an artist, a police officer or fire fighter, or other interesting individual who could share his or her talents with the kids.

Or you could go on a birthday party field trip that provides built-in activities: visit a natural history or science museum, an aquarium or zoo, go to a movie or children's play, visit a children's museum or discovery center, go out for hot dogs or hamburgers, go to a kid's race-car track or take a train ride, visit a Laser Tag or video game parlor, visit a water or theme park, go behind the scenes at an ice cream or candy factory, or take the kids out to the ballgame.

Last but not least, you might show a favorite video at the party that ties in with your theme to keep the kids entertained for an hour or two. You could even use the video to set the stage for the party theme.

Whatever you choose to do, activity time will provide lots of fun for your party guests. Time to get busy!

Amazing Swami

Mystify the party crowd with the Amazing Swami magic act! No matter what card you choose, the Swami always knows.

Materials

* Deck of cards
* Telephone
* Friend to play the part of Swami

WHAT TO DO

Before the party begins, arrange a code with a friend who will not be at the party and who will play Swami. Tell Swami that when you call on the telephone during the party, you'll say: "Could I speak to the Amazing Swami?" This will alert Swami that it's time for the trick. Ask someone from the group to pick a card from the deck and show it to everyone (including you). Tell the group you are going to telephone the Amazing Swami and have Swami guess the card. Then, when you say to Swami on the phone, "Could I speak to the Amazing Swami?" Swami should immediately begin counting slowly from ace to king. When Swami reaches the number you have seen on the card, you quickly interrupt Swami with a second sentence: "Hello, Swami!" That interruption lets Swami know what number is on the chosen card. Swami immediately begins to recite the four suits. When Swami says the correct suit, you quickly interrupt again and say, "Tell my friend the card he has picked from the deck." Hand the phone over to the guest so he can listen to Swami reveal the card!

BIKE BAZAAR

Let the kids perk up the bike-a-thon with colorful decorations, then have a parade!

MATERIALS

* Crepe paper streamers in a variety of colors
* Tape
* Colorful playing cards or baseball cards
* Clothespins
* Spoke beads
* Pipe cleaners
* Metallic ribbon
* Pom-poms
* Windmills
* Other bicycle accessories

WHAT TO DO

Ask the guests to bring their bikes to the Bike Bazaar. Provide them with lots of things to decorate the bikes with, as mentioned above. Wind the crepe paper streamers among the spokes of the bike wheels and around the frame, taping

down the loose ends. Add ribbons or pom-poms to the handlebars. Clip cards onto the spokes to make a clicking noise. Have awards for each guest's creativity, such as "Funniest," "Most Overloaded," "Best Decorated," "Most Bizarre," "Most Elegant," "Fanciest," "Most Likely to Fall Apart Right Away," and so on. Then have a parade, riding the bikes around the neighborhood.

BLACK HOLE

Will the kids reach into the Black Hole or will fear of the unknown overcome them?

MATERIALS

* 10 milk cartons, small boxes, or cardboard cans
* 10 large old socks
* 10 weird-feeling items that will fit inside the boxes or cans
* Paper and pencils

WHAT TO DO

Find some strange-feeling items that will fit in the boxes or cans. For example, you might use a slice of pizza, the packaged slimy stuff available at the toy store, an ice cube, a square of Jell-O, a Koosh ball, some underwear, a rubber spider, a flower, a lock of hair, some fake plastic vomit, a wet rag, or some of the Gooshy Goos included in this chapter. Place one item in each box or can and pull a sock up over the can, with the opening of the sock at the top. Be sure you can't see the item inside. Have the kids sit in a circle. Pass the sock boxes around the circle one at a time, allowing each guest time to feel what's inside and react. Have them write down what the item is, or wait until everyone has felt the item, then let them guess what it is as a group.

BLIND WALK

Kids love to close their eyes and try to find their way around. Here are several activities you can do during a Blind Walk.

MATERIALS

* Blindfolds
* Small obstacles, such as a pillow, a box, a toy

WHAT TO DO

First pair up the kids. Blindfold one child in each pair. Have the partners lead their blindfolded pals around the house or yard on a chosen path, using only their voices and without holding their hands. Set some obstacles in the way and have the partners guide the blindfolded kids around them. If anyone stumbles, trips, or bumps into an obstacle, the couple has to start over. The couple that makes it all the way through without an accident wins.

Then blindfold the kids one at a time and have them walk around a smaller obstacle course all by themselves, without tripping, stumbling, or falling. The one who makes it through without a mishap wins.

BOX CARS

All you need for this fun activity are cardboard boxes big enough to fit around small bodies.

MATERIALS

* 1 large box to fit around each child
* X-acto knife or other sharp knife
* Tempera or poster paints
* Black felt-tip pen
* Stapler

WHAT TO DO

Cut off the bottom and top of each box, leaving the four sides intact. Cut a small slit on two sides of each box where the kids can fit their hands. Have the kids paint the sides of the boxes, adding details and designs to create a race car, bus, truck, fire engine, police car, or whatever they want. Use the black felt-tip pen or black paint to outline the colors and give them definition. Use the box top or bottom to create wheels and staple them into place on two sides of the car. When finished and dry, have the kids step inside their vehicles, hold onto the handle slits, and take off. You can use cardboard boxes to create a number of different "vehicles" for fun; turn them into robots, monsters, TV sets, forts, anything you like!

BUBBLE MACHINE

Spend the afternoon blowing, chasing, and popping bubbles. There are lots of ways to turn your party into a Bubble Machine.

MATERIALS

* $1/3$ cup Ivory dish soap, dishwashing detergent, or baby shampoo
* $1 1/3$ cups water
* 2 teaspoons sugar or glycerin
* 1 drop food coloring
* Pan or bucket
* Paper cups or shallow pan
* Blowers, such as straws with the ends cut off diagonally, pipe cleaners twisted into circular shapes, strawberry baskets from the grocery store, coat hangers twisted into large circles, heavy string, old glasses with the lenses taken out, small paper cups with the bottoms cut out

WHAT TO DO

Combine soap, water, sugar or glycerin, and food coloring in a pan or bucket. Pour into individual paper cups and distribute to the kids, or pour into a shallow pan for the group to share. Let the kids experiment with the bubble blowers listed above.

CANDY LEIS

Fun to make, fun to wear, and especially fun to eat!

MATERIALS

* 16 pieces of different kinds of candy in wrappers twisted at each end for each child
* 16 (6-inch) lengths of different colored curl-type ribbon for each child
* Scissors

WHAT TO DO

Divide up the candy and the pre-cut ribbon for each guest. Have them arrange the candy in a pattern of their choosing. Show them how to attach one candy to another by placing one wrapped candy beside another wrapped candy, with the twisted ends overlapping each other. Tie a piece of ribbon to the overlapped twisted ends so they connect. Repeat with each candy until all sixteen pieces are connected, and the first candy is connected to the last candy to form a necklace or lei. Using scissors, curl the ribbon ends all the way around the lei to make it even more festive. Slip the lei over your head and do the hula!

CHOCOLATE CRITTERS

Make 'em and then eat 'em!

MATERIALS

* 1 cup chocolate chips for each child
* 1 small sealable plastic bag for each child
* Candy decorations, such as sprinkles, Red Hots, stars, confetti
* Frosting
* Nuts, cereal, granola
* Waxed paper

WHAT TO DO

Place waxed paper at each child's place at the table. Fill plastic bags with chocolate chips and seal bag. Place in microwave and heat on high for two minutes until melted. (Your oven may require a few more seconds, but don't let the chocolate get too hot.) Remove from oven and cut a small piece off the corner of a bag. Let the kids squeeze the chocolate onto the waxed paper, making little bugs, creatures, critters, and monsters. Sprinkle on decorations, or place on the decorations to make eyes, nose, and mouth. For extra fun, fill plastic bags with colored frosting, cut the tip off one corner, and let the kids squeeze out the frosting onto the critters. Or lay out little piles of nuts, cereal, or granola, and let the kids cover them with the melted chocolate to make creepy critters. Let them eat what they make.

COMIC STRIPS

Need a good laugh? Make these creative Comic Strips with the kids!

MATERIALS

* A collection of Sunday funnies
* Strips of white poster board to use as comic panels
* White paper
* Scissors and felt-tip pen for each guest
* Glue

WHAT TO DO

Collect a pile of Sunday comic strips before the party. Have the kids sit at the table and give them each a white poster board strip to work with. Spread the comic pages over the table and let the kids choose the cartoon characters they want to use in their comic strips. Have them cut out a variety of characters and scenes, and arrange them on the poster board to tell a story. Show them how to divide up the panels, and how to cut out speech balloons from the white paper. Glue the characters and speech balloons onto the poster board. Have the kids write what they want in the speech balloons and then share their comic strips with the rest of the group.

CREATIVE CONSTRUCTION

Here are three ways for the kids to create their own construction projects.

MATERIALS

* Frozen peas
* Toothpicks
* Thin wooden skewers
* Styrofoam chips
* Wooden ice cream sticks
* Play-Doh, modeling clay, or Baker's Clay (page 213)

WHAT TO DO

Offer the kids several opportunities for creating their own construction projects. All you need are two items: building materials and the stuff that sticks them together. Supply the kids with frozen peas and toothpicks for one type of construction. They can munch on the peas as they work. Then give them Styrofoam chips from packaging or hobby stores and use them with thin wooden skewers cut in half, and the sharp ends cut off. Finally provide ice cream sticks and dough or clay, and have the kids put together their own creative constructions. Award prizes to all participants in a wide range of categories: Most Bizarre, Funniest, Tallest, Longest, Biggest, Most Likely to Fall Apart, and so on.

DINOSAUR EGG HUNT

Here's an unusual twist on the traditional treasure hunt. This time the kids discover prehistoric dinosaur eggs—with a surprise inside!

MATERIALS

* 2 cups sand
* 1 cup cornstarch
* 1 1/2 cups water
* Small plastic dinosaurs

WHAT TO DO

Mix sand, cornstarch, and water in a large pan on the stove, and heat until warm. Shape a portion of the warm sand mixture around a small plastic dinosaur, molding it into an egg shape. Set aside, and allow to dry and harden. Repeat, making enough dinosaur eggs for each child. When the "eggs" are firm, place them around

the yard, slightly hidden from view. Handle the eggs carefully; they are fragile. Have the kids hunt for the dinosaur eggs, then let them crack the eggs open to find the surprise inside!

FACE IT!

Be whatever you want to be with Face It! All you need is imagination and a few basic materials to make your amazing transformation!

MATERIALS

* Large rectangular sheets of cardboard or poster board
* Paint, felt-tip pens, crayons, puffy paints
* Makeup or face paints
* Polaroid camera

WHAT TO DO

Cut cardboard from large appliance boxes or use large sheets of poster board. You'll need one sheet for each child. Cut a hole about the size of a child's face near the top of the length-wise end of the cardboard. Tell the kids that's where the face will go and to use it as a guide for the rest of the body. Have the kids draw a body outline on the cardboard of a favorite cartoon character, superhero, animal, monster, or other creature. Color in the body with paints, felt-tip pens, or crayons to add detail. Prop up the cardboard between two chairs, back-to-back, to keep it from falling over. Have a child stand behind the sheet of cardboard with his face sticking through the hole. Take a picture of him or her as Mickey Mouse, Power Ranger, or the Swamp Thing.

FACE PAINTING

Create your own Face Painting makeup and see who can make up the funniest face.

MATERIALS

* Small bowls, paper cups, or a muffin tin
* 1 teaspoon cold cream per bowl
* 1 teaspoon cornstarch per bowl

- * ¹/₂ teaspoon water per bowl
- * 3 drops food coloring per bowl
- * Eyebrow pencils
- * Lip liners
- * Eye shadows
- * Cheek blush
- * Small paintbrushes or cotton swabs
- * Sequins, glitter, sparkly makeup

WHAT TO DO

Make up several bowls of face painting makeup in a variety of colors, combining the cold cream, corn starch, water, and food color. Design a funny face on paper or directly on the face using eye pencils and lip liners. Fill in with the small paintbrushes using the cold cream mixture. Take pictures and award prizes for the funniest face, along with other categories you come up with.

FASHION FUN

Make your own ready-to-wear and turn a plain old T-shirt into a work of fashionable art.

MATERIALS

- * T-shirt for each child
- * Cardboard
- * Puffy paints, fabric paints, permanent felt-tip pens
- * Glitter, sequins, press-on appliqués, iron-on fabric

WHAT TO DO

Either have the kids bring a white T-shirt to the party or buy some inexpensive shirts for everyone. Cut out squares or T-shirt shapes from the cardboard and slip the cardboard shapes inside the T-shirts to make the fabric smooth. Tape the back of each T-shirt to the underside of the cardboard to keep it from sliding and to keep it taut (but not stretched), or tack each T-shirt to the cardboard with thumbtacks. Let the kids make a design on the front of their T-shirts with the paints and pens. They can create their own designs, or you can purchase iron-on designs ahead of time and let the kids choose what they want. Add decorations with glitter, sequins, iron-ons, and other accessories. Allow the shirt to dry. Then have the kids model their new creations.

FINGER FUNNIES

Fill the little fingers with funny little figures. Here are two varieties.

OLD MACDONALD'S FARM

MATERIALS

* 1 garden glove for each child
* 5 medium-sized pom-poms—2 pinks, 1 yellow, 1 brown, 1 white for each child
* Colored felt
* 1 yellow feather for each child
* 1 small farmer hat (available at hobby stores) for each child
* 10 small plastic wiggly eyes for each child
* Glue or glue gun
* Permanent felt-tip pen

WHAT TO DO

Old MacDonald's Farm works well as a theme for the glove puppet, but you can use your imagination and some favorite children's books to come up with additional themes, such as the Three Little Pigs, Peter Pan, or Snow White. For the farm theme, give a clean garden glove to each child at the table, and set out materials. Let the kids glue on the pom-poms—the pinks for the farmer and the pig, yellow for the chick, brown for the cow, and white for the sheep. Cut out ears, noses, beaks, cow horns, and bow tie from felt. Glue the felt pieces and the feather on to the pom-poms. Allow the glove to dry, then sing "Old MacDonald Had a Farm" and act it out with the puppet glove.

MINI-MONSTERS

MATERIALS

* 1 tight-fitting knit or cloth glove for each child
* Scraps of yarn
* Scraps of felt
* 10 small plastic wiggly eyes for each child
* Glue or glue gun
* Permanent felt-tip pen

WHAT TO DO

Cut the fingers off each glove at the knuckle to get five glove tips. Glue wiggly eyes on to the glove tips. Cut out monster features, such as mouths, tongues, ears, tails, and so on from the felt and glue to the glove tips. Add yarn hair at the top. Put the glove tips on fingers and make up a story with your Mini-Monsters.

FUNNY FACE

Make portraits of the guests that will have them laughing in no time. Then let them take home their "twins."

MATERIALS

* Large, sturdy balloon for each child
* Tagboard
* Permanent felt-tip pens or puffy paints
* Yarn, wiggle eyes, sequins, hats, and other accessories

WHAT TO DO

Blow up a balloon for each child and tie off the end. Cut tagboard into a large circle, and shape into a pair of feet. Cut a slit down the middle and insert the tied end of balloon into the slit. Tape the balloon end to the bottom of the tagboard feet. Now you have a balloon head sitting on a pair of feet. Give a balloon head to each child. Write the names of the kids on individual sheets of paper and drop them into a bowl or hat. Without revealing what name they have drawn, have them pick a piece of paper from the hat. They must make a "twin" for the person whose name they chose, using felt tip pens, puffy paints, yarn for hair, and other accessories. When everyone is finished, display the Funny Faces for all to see and let each kid guess which one is his or her "twin." Let them take home their twins at the end of the party.

GALAXY GAZERS

Use these Galaxy Gazers at night to see the stars and constellations.

MATERIALS

* Round oatmeal carton for each child
* Poster board
* Constellation chart
* Straight pin
* Flashlight for each guest

WHAT TO DO

Collect oatmeal cartons for each guest, or ask them to bring their own. Buy them each a small novelty flashlight or ask them to bring one from home. At a work table, have the kids cut a circle from the bottom of the oatmeal carton, leaving a 1/4-inch rim. Make several circles from the poster board a little larger than the circle you cut from the bottom of the carton. Using a star chart, make some simple constellations by poking pin holes into the cut-out poster-board circles. Each pinhole creates a "star." Copy your favorite constellations, or create new ones shaped like animals, monsters, or cartoon characters. Have the kids lie down on the floor with their Galaxy Gazers and the extra circles, and give them each a flashlight.

Then turn out the lights and tell them to place a circle over the bottom of the carton. Put the flashlight into the other end of the oatmeal box, turn it on, and aim it at the ceiling. Watch the stars light up the night!

GHOSTS AND GOBLINS

Make these scary creatures that can float from the ceiling or have them sit on the shelf. It's magical how they these ghosts keep their figures!

MATERIALS

* White glue
* Water
* Foil
* Cheesecloth
* Paper cup
* Waxed paper
* Pair of wiggly eyes or tiny black pom-poms for each child
* Elastic thread

WHAT TO DO

For each child, mix 1 teaspoon of white glue with 2 teaspoons water until a milk-like consistency is achieved, and set aside in individual small bowls. Form foil on top of an upside-down paper cup to make a ghost head. Place cup with foil on waxed paper. Cut the cheesecloth into 6-inch squares (or larger for bigger cups). Dip a square of cheesecloth into the glue mixture and squeeze out excess. Drape over the foil head and cup to make a ghost form, smoothing and shaping as you go. Stick on wiggly eyes or tiny black pom-poms for eyes. Allow to dry. Remove the cup and foil head from under the ghost. Thread elastic through the ghost head and hang from the ceiling, or set the ghost on a shelf.

GOOSHY GOO

In a kids' perfect world, the motto is "The messier, the better." Here are some recipes for handfuls of gooshy, gooey substances.

GOOP

MATERIALS

* 1/2 cup cornstarch
* 1/4 cup water
* Few drops of food coloring
* Sealable plastic sandwich bags

WHAT TO DO

Combine cornstarch, water, and food coloring in a bowl. Mix together. (Hint: If you try to mix the Goop too quickly it will resist. If you mix it slowly, it will behave more like a liquid. You may need a tablespoon or two more water if it doesn't eventually liquefy.) When completely mixed, pour small amounts of the Goop into plastic bags and seal closed. Let the kids handle the bags of Goop first, exploring the properties of the mixture. They'll feel the Goop get firm if they squeeze hard, and they'll feel it turn soft and liquefy if they let it relax in their hands. Then let them take the Goop out of the plastic bag for hands-on fun. This is messy, so give the kids smocks and cover the table with newspapers.

KOOL-AID DOUGH

MATERIALS

* 2 1/2 cups flour
* 1/2 cup salt
* 2 packages unsweetened Kool-Aid
* 3 tablespoons cooking oil
* 2 cups boiling water

WHAT TO DO

Mix together the flour, salt, and Kool-Aid mix. Add the oil and water, and mix well with a spoon. When the dough has cooled, knead it a few times. Give a handful of dough to each guest and let them create whatever they want with the colorful mixture.

SMOOSHY STUFF

MATERIALS

* 2 cups white glue
* 1 1/2 cups water
* Food coloring
* 2 teaspoons borax

* 2/3 cup warm water
* Food coloring

WHAT TO DO

In a large container, mix glue and water together, along with a few drops of food coloring. In a separate container, dissolve the borax in the warm water and mix well. Mix the borax solution with the glue solution and let the kids watch what happens to the mixture. Pass out handfuls of the Smooshy Stuff to the kids so they can explore the unusual properties of the mixture, which feels cold, wet, and strange. Play with Smooshy Stuff outside and give the kids smocks to protect their clothing.

SQUEEZERS

MATERIALS

* 1 cup water
* 1 cup flour
* 1 1/2 cups salt
* Tempera paint
* Squeeze bottles
* Large sheets of paper

WHAT TO DO

Mix water, flour, and salt in a bowl until smooth. Pour into squeeze bottles. Add tempera paint to bottles to create different colors. Provide large sheets of paper for the kids and let them squeeze the paint onto the paper in any design they want. Let the artwork dry before sending it home.

TASTY DOUGH

MATERIALS

* 1 can frosting
* 1 1/2 cups powdered sugar
* 1 cup peanut butter
* Kitchen accessories

WHAT TO DO

Mix the ingredients in a bowl. Knead into a firm dough. Separate the dough into equal amounts for each kid to play with, using kitchen items such as cookie cutters, rolling pins, plastic silverware, or a garlic press.

HAIRY HEAD

Watch the hair sprout on this very funny face!

MATERIALS

* Plate for each child
* Sawdust
* Knee-high nylon or a leg cut off of old pantyhose for each child
* Grass seeds
* Glue
* Pair of wiggly eyes for each child
* Rubber bands
* 20-gauge plastic coated wire
* Liter-size plastic soda bottle with both ends cut off for each child
* Accessories, such as eyelashes, ribbons, bows, hats, wire glasses

WHAT TO DO

Place a plate on the table and place plastic soda bottle container on top of plate. Pack sawdust into the container, filling it almost to the top. Pour a handful of seeds on top of the sawdust. Carefully slide the nylon over the container and plate so that the nylon's opening is at the plate end. Flip the container over, and remove the plate. Push down the sawdust with your fist, while slowly lifting out the soda bottle container. (Save the container to use as a display stand for Hairy Head.) Pack the sawdust down and tie the nylon closed. Dip the head of sawdust into a bowl of water and let it soak for a few minutes. Remove from water and squeeze out excess. Turn the ball over and shape the head, which should be moldable. Gently pull a small clump of sawdust out from the middle of the face for the nose and twist it off with a rubber band. Press and shape the rest of the face. Glue on eyes, glasses, eyelashes, a hat, or whatever the kids wish. Set on a stand, such as the soda bottle container. Send the heads home with the kids and tell them to keep them damp and near indirect sunlight over the next few days, and to watch Hairy Head grow hair!

HANSEL AND GRETEL'S HOUSE

It's hard to know which is more fun—making the candy house for Hansel and Gretel—or eating it up!

MATERIALS

* Small cardboard box
* Piece of cardboard
* Graham crackers
* Royal icing, seven-minute icing, or regular icing
* Variety of small candies, cookies, lollipops, licorice

WHAT TO DO

Set a small cardboard box on the kitchen table. Cut out a roof from the extra piece of cardboard and tape or glue to the top of the box to form a

house. Let the kids cover the house and roof with frosting. Stick on the graham crackers until the house is covered. Then stick candies all over the house, using the frosting as glue. Let the kids be creative with their designs. When the house is finished, let the kids eat their architectural creation.

MARBLE MANIA

It's surprising how beautiful these marbleized items turn out. The kids will love them!

MATERIALS

* Objects to marbleize, such as small white boxes, smooth stones, note cards, small wooden blocks, glass or plastic eggs, shells
* Small bottles of enamel paint
* Disposable bowls, buckets, or pans
* Water
* Toothpicks
* Paper towels
* Old bacon tongs

WHAT TO DO

Collect items that will hold enamel paint when they are marbleized, as mentioned above. Fill disposable bowls, buckets, or pans with water deep enough to submerge the items you wish to marbleize. For example, use a shallow pan for paper, a bowl for stones. Drop a few drops of two or three colors of enamel paint onto the surface of the water. Swirl the paint gently with toothpicks to make a marble design. Quickly pick up an item with the tongs and dip it all the way into the water and out again. The item will be beautifully marbleized! Allow to dry on paper towels. Blot the surface of the water with paper towels to remove the leftover paint. Change water every fourth or fifth time.

MODEL BEHAVIOR

Dress for success and model your new look for the video or Polaroid camera.

MATERIALS

* Dress-up clothes (the fancier the better)
* Accessories, such as hats, gloves, furs, wigs, scarves, and shoes
* Makeup
* Jewelry
* Video or Polaroid camera

WHAT TO DO

Provide the kids with a box full of dress-up clothes. You can pick up inexpensive items such as silky dresses, sequined gowns, party frocks, and even chiffon lingerie at the thrift store. Add accessories such as big hats, bouncy wigs, white gloves, high spike-heeled shoes, and jewelry. Then have the kids do one another's makeup—extra thick and vampy—and style their hair in a fancy, pouffy fashion. Provide some kind of ramp or walkway for the kids to model their new looks and videotape them as they walk. Or have them pose for still pictures using the Polaroid camera.

MYSTERIOUS MESSAGE

Amaze your guests with Mysterious Messages from the spirits.

MATERIALS

* Fish bowl, round vase, or other similar bowl
* Small votive candle
* Dry ice (optional)
* White paper
* Lemon juice or milk
* Small paintbrushes

WHAT TO DO

Prepare the "crystal ball" by setting a small candle inside a fish bowl or other round bowl. Set dry ice around the candle if you like, which will add a spooky mist. Give each guest a small sheet of paper and a paintbrush. Ask them to make up a secret fortune for an assigned child at the party. Have them write the fortune on the paper with a paintbrush dipped in lemon juice or milk. When everyone is finished, have each child hold his or her fortune over the crystal ball. Watch the secret message appear as if by magic!

PHOTO PAPER DOLLS

Make your own paper dolls that look just like you!

MATERIALS

* Store-bought paper doll or one made from tagboard for each child
* Wallet-sized school picture of each child
* Felt-tip pens, crayons, puffy paints

WHAT TO DO

Ask the kids to bring a snapshot of themselves, like the ones taken at school. Have them cut out their heads from the photographs and glue them onto the paper doll bodies, to create personalized paper dolls. Let them decorate the bodies and create clothes for the paper dolls to

wear using the pens, crayons, and paints. Then let them play with their "just like me" dolls!

PIPELINE

They say plumbers make a lot of money putting pipes together, but I'll bet they don't have as much fun as this!

MATERIALS

* Lengths of straight plastic pipe used for sprinklers and water systems, cut into varying lengths from a few inches to a few feet (available at hardware and home improvement stores)
* Several connection pieces of plastic pipe, diameter 125 type, l-shaped, t-shaped, and x-shaped
* Water, sand, marbles, round candies
* Funnels

WHAT TO DO

Supply the guests with a collection of plastic pipes in a variety of shapes and lengths and let them create whatever they want as a group. You might suggest that they start with a base or foundation, then construct it upward to make a waterway. When they've finished their construction and all the pipe pieces are connected, have them test it by placing a funnel at the highest end and filling it with water, to see if the water runs all the way to the other end. If it doesn't, let them figure out how to correct the problem and try again. You can also test the pipeline with sand, marbles, and round candies if using large-diameter pipe.

POPCORN EXPLOSION

The kids will be shocked—and delighted—when they witness this exciting Popcorn Explosion. And of course they get to eat the outcome!

MATERIALS

* Popcorn popper, the automatic kind (not an air popper)
* Popcorn
* Oil
* Large clean sheet

WHAT TO DO

Spread out the sheet on a large area in the room and gather the kids around the edge, but not on the sheet itself. Tell the kids the sheet is a volcano about to erupt so they must not cross the border. Set the popcorn popper in the middle of the sheet, add oil and fill with popcorn kernels, according to package directions. Plug in the popcorn popper but do NOT put on the lid. The excitement builds as the popcorn kernels heat up and begin to pop up in the air and onto the sheet. When the popcorn is done and the sheet is covered with popcorn, unplug the popper and remove it from the center of the sheet. Then let the kids attack the popcorn!

POP-UP CLOWN

The kids can make their own surprise Pop-Up Clowns to take home after the party.

MATERIALS

* Paper cups
* Pencils
* Small white socks
* Permanent felt-tip pens or fabric paints
* Small Styrofoam balls
* Rubber bands or string
* Glue

WHAT TO DO

With the paper cups upside-down, make a small hole at the bottom of the paper cup and insert a pencil, point-side down, into the cup. Stick a Styrofoam ball on the tip of the pencil. Have the kids color the white socks with permanent felt-tip pens or fabric paints, leaving the toe white. Cover the Styrofoam ball, then the cup, with the decorated sock. Tie a rubber band or some string around the sock-covered ball, leaving the bottom open. Draw faces on the "heads" of the socks. Then reach into the sock at the opening, grasp the pencil, and pull it gently down. The clown's head will disappear into the cup. With a brisk movement, push the pencil up and watch the clown pop out of the cup!

SALT SCAPE

The salt magically transforms the colored chalk into a beautiful landscape!

MATERIALS

* Empty baby food jar for each child
* Small plastic bowl for each child
* 1 sheet of construction paper for each child
* Colored chalk, large sidewalk-size preferred
* Salt
* Glue
* Ribbon

WHAT TO DO

Cover the table with newspaper. Give each child an empty baby food jar, a plastic bowl, a sheet of construction paper, and a piece of chalk. Pour some salt onto the construction paper. Have the kids rub the chalk over the salt and see it change the salt into the chalk's color! When everyone has rubbed the chalk into the salt to form the colored "sand," have them pour the sand into their own small bowls. Let each child pour a small amount of his or her color into the baby food jar to make a thin layer on the bottom. Pass the bowls around the table so each child gets a chance to add layers of different colored "sand" to their jars. When the jars are completely filled, glue the lids on, tie a ribbon around the tops, and let the guests take their Salt Scapes home.

SIXTIES SHIRTS

Go back to the sixties and create a collection of hippie outfits, using tie-dye techniques and easy batik.

MATERIALS

* White cotton T-shirt for each child
* Rubber bands
* Crayons
* Paraffin
* Brush
* Fabric dye
* Paper towels
* Iron
* Muffin tin

WHAT TO DO

To turn your T-shirts into unique works of sixties art, ask the kids to bring white cotton T-shirts to the party, or provide them yourself. Have the kids grasp a section of T-shirt, preferably in the center of the front or back, and pull it

up with their hands. Tie rubber bands tightly around the wadded-up sections. Repeat in as many places as they like. Dip the banded knobs of fabric into fabric dye mixed according to the package directions. Squeeze out excess color, remove the rubber bands, dip in other colors, if desired, and dry the shirts in the dryer. Melt paraffin and paint it over the dyed circles on the shirt. When the wax is dry, wrinkle the shirt, and dip the entire shirt into another color of dye. Iron off wax using paper towels on both sides of the design, and dry completely.

Or peel crayons and place them in an old cupcake tin, along with a small square of paraffin. Melt over a double-boiler or a hot tray. Let the kids carefully paint designs on the shirts with the melted crayons. When the waxed color is dry, wrinkle up the shirt and dip it into fabric dye. Wring out, place T-shirt on an ironing board, and layer two to three sheets of paper towel on both sides of the waxed sections. Press with a hot iron to have the paper towels absorb the wax, leaving the color in the shirt. Continue ironing, using more paper towels until the shirt is free of wax. Dry shirt if wet. It's now ready to wear with your love beads and bell-bottoms!

STORK WALKERS

These high-top Stork Walkers make the kids feel ten feet tall.

MATERIALS

* 2 large coffee cans for each child
* Acrylic paint
* Brushes
* Hammer and nails
* 5 yards of rope for each child

WHAT TO DO

Collect a bunch of coffee cans from friends and neighbors, or ask the kids to save and bring two cans each to the party. Let the kids paint the cans with acrylic paints and allow them to dry. Have an adult punch a hole on either side of a can, near the bottom. Thread a two-foot piece of rope through the holes, and tie the ends together so the rope won't come out. Tie a second piece of rope about 3 feet long to the rope looped through the can. Repeat for all the cans.

Have the kids step on the cans and, holding the ends of the 3-foot ropes, walk around on their Stork Walkers. Set up an obstacle course for the kids to walk over, around, on, and through. For more fun, wear an old pair of long pants to cover the can and ropes.

STORYBOOK THEATER

Have the kids work together to construct the Storybook Theater, then let them put on a show!

* 1 large appliance box
* X-acto knife or other sharp knife
* Tempera paint
* Scrap fabric large enough to use as a theater curtain
* Yarn or ribbon

WHAT TO DO

Cut the back off the large box so the kids can get inside. Make a large rectangular opening in the top half of the box to form the stage area. Have the kids paint the front and sides of the box to look like a theater or television set. On the inside of the box, staple two pieces of fabric across the top of the opening to serve as curtains. Tie them back with ribbon or yarn, and poke holes on either side of the opening to tie up the ribbons (or just flip the curtain up when it's show time). Have the kids put on a show using cloth puppets, dolls, stuffed animals, stick puppets, shadow puppets, or themselves. Videotape the performance and show it to the kids when they're finished with the play.

SUPER STICKERS

The guests can make their own Super Stickers just the way they want them. Then watch them stick!

MATERIALS

* Comic books, Sunday funnies, cartoon strips, and other pictures of cartoon characters
* Clear Con-Tact paper
* Scissors for each guest

WHAT TO DO

Lay out a selection of cartoons and pictures of cartoon characters on the table. Cut a foot of Con-Tact paper for each child. Tell the kids to cut out several of their favorite characters. Have them peel off the backside of the Con-Tact paper just halfway, and place the cartoon characters face down on the sticky side of the Con-Tact paper. Re-cover the sticky part with the backing. Have the kids cut out the cartoon characters from the Con-Tact paper leaving a 1/4-inch margin all around the figure. Now they have their own stickers.

Peel off the other half of the Con-Tact paper and have the kids lay more cut-out cartoon characters face down on one quarter of the sticky paper. Fold over the other quarter of the sticky paper, sticky sides together. Have the kids cut out the cartoon figures, again leaving a 1/4-inch margin around the outside. This time have them dampen the stickers to make them stick when placed on the refrigerator, bathtub, or other metal, glass, or porcelain surface.

SURPRISE BAGS

After the big surprise, the kids can make these Surprise Bags filled with magic dust.

MATERIALS

* Two paper lunch bags for each child
* Straight pin

* Confetti
* Tissues
* Glue

WHAT TO DO

Before the party begins, prepare one surprise bag. Using a straight pin, stick a bunch of holes in the bottom of one of the bags. Put a handful of confetti in the bottom of the bag with the holes. Insert a second bag into the first and smooth into a close fit, leaving 1/2 inch of the second bag sticking up above the first bag. Fold the top of the second bag over the first bag so it looks like one bag.

At the party, present the bag to the audience and show them you have nothing but an empty paper bag. Ask one of the guests to place a plain white tissue into the bag. Tell them you will turn the tissue into shredded colorful confetti, just by blowing up the bag and popping it. Then blow up the bag, twist off the end, and pop the bag. Watch the surprise when the confetti comes bursting out of the bottom! Then teach the kids how to make their own Surprise Bags.

TREASURE OR TRASH?

One kid's trash is sometimes another kid's treasure. Add the element of surprise, and you have a crazy activity called Treasure or Trash!

MATERIALS

* An unwanted toy, article of clothing, or other item brought by each guest to the party, wrapped
* Paper and pencil

WHAT TO DO

Ask each guest to bring an unwanted item from home, such as a sweater that's too big, a shirt that's too ugly, a toy that's too young, or a tape that's too nerdy (the less appealing the better—and funnier). Ask the guests to wrap up the discarded item in fancy paper and bring it to the party, unmarked. Place all the packages on a table. Gather the kids together and have them draw numbers from a bowl or hat. The person who gets number one has first choice. He or she can choose a gift from the assortment on the table. After a gift is chosen, he or she sits down and opens the gift up for all to see and enjoy. Then, guest number two gets a chance to pick a gift from the wrapped pile, or he or she may take away the gift from a player who has already opened a gift—it's his or her choice. When all the gifts are selected and opened, let the kids share their stories about how each item was chosen for the party.

FUN PARTY FOODS

fter all the party fun and excitement, the kids will be more than ready for refreshments. Whether it's cake and ice cream, snacks and treats, or special mini-meals, be sure to serve a variety of creative foods to keep your guests from overloading on sweets. All you need is a little imagination to turn your simple servings into festive foods!

You can make the birthday cake the centerpiece on the table, or it can become part of the party fun. Let the kids help decorate a cupcake, a slice of cake, or even the whole cake, with tubes of frosting, colorful sprinkles, small candies, and tiny toys. Or have the kids help create some of the other snacks and treats, so the food doubles as a party activity.

Serve the cake and ice cream after you have offered some fancy snacks, tasty treats, mini-meals, and mouthwatering drinks, and offer a variety of choices to provide for individual tastes. Present all the edibles on decorative plates with matching cups, forks, spoons, and napkins, all tied into your birthday theme. Or serve the food in unique containers, such as carved-out melons or oranges, coffee mugs or champagne glasses, bread bowls or cream puff shells, plastic eggs or beach pails.

Here are some unique recipes for special party refreshments that will make your celebration a piece of cake!

SUPER SNACKS

ALL-YOU-CAN-EAT BUFFET

The kids will love this all-you-can-take and all-you-can-eat buffet, anytime of the day! Try other buffet ideas, for example, using tacos, pizza, sandwiches, or hot dogs and hamburgers.

INGREDIENTS

* A variety of cereals poured into a number of separate bowls

* A variety of fruit, such as strawberries, cantaloupe, raisins, bananas, and berries, cut into slices as necessary and placed in separate bowls
* Milk

WHAT TO DO

Let your child pick out eight to ten favorite cereals from the store. Pour them into individual bowls and line them up on the counter or table. Prepare the fruit, place in separate bowls, and set on the table. Give each guest a bowl and a spoon and let him dip into any of the breakfast offerings to create an original cereal-and-fruit dish. Add milk and enjoy.

BANANA BUTTER BUNS

This might be the strangest snack you've ever made. But it's also one of the tastiest—at least to kids!

INGREDIENTS

* 4 ripe bananas
* 4 hot dog buns or flour tortillas
* $1/2$ cup chunky peanut butter
* $1/4$ cup raisins or jam
* $1/4$ cup shredded coconut and chopped nuts (optional)

WHAT TO DO

Place peeled bananas in hot dog buns. Spread peanut butter on either side. Add raisins, jam, coconut, and nuts, if desired. Heat in microwave for 30 to 45 seconds, or until warmed.

Makes 4

COLOSSAL COOKIE

Instead of a cake, why not make a Colossal Cookie and surprise your guests with the size! You can alter the shape of the cookie to suit your party theme—make it a teddy bear, a star, a sign, an alphabet letter, or anything!

INGREDIENTS

* Favorite chocolate chip, oatmeal raisin, sugar, or peanut butter cookie recipe
* Piece of cardboard, the size of a large pizza
* Foil or fancy gift wrap
* Tubes of frosting with decorator tips

WHAT TO DO

Preheat oven according to recipe directions. Make your favorite sturdy cookie dough. Shape all of the dough into a large circle or shape of choice on a large, well-greased cookie sheet. Bake until lightly browned all over and firm in the middle. (This should take about 5 to 10 minutes longer than the recipe states.) When cool, slip the cookie onto cardboard covered with foil or gift wrap. Decorate with frosting to outline cookie, make designs, and write the birthday child's name in the center. Use as a centerpiece until serving time, then break off chunks and pass them out to the guests.

Serves 8 to 10

MIXIN' MUNCHIES

Let the guests mix together whatever they want from the Mixin' Munchies Bar.

INGREDIENTS

* 1/2 cup each miniature shredded wheat cereal, Cheerios, Rice Krispies, (and other favorite cereals), raisins, dried fruit pieces, peanuts, broken pretzels, corn chips, seeds, banana chips, apple chips, granola, cookie crumbs, shredded coconut, carob chips, and other trail-mix-type foods
* Small bowls

WHAT TO DO

Collect a variety of trail mix items, such as the ones suggested above, and pour them into separate small bowls. Line the bowls up along a counter or table. Give guests a small bowl and spoon, let them walk around the table gathering whatever trail mix items they want into their own bowls. Offer the kids plastic spoons to eat the Mixin' Munchies right from their bowls, or pour the mix into plastic lunch bags and let them use their fingers.

Serves 8 to 10

PAINTED COOKIES

Creative kids can "paint" their own cookies before they gobble them up! You can also paint slices of bread the same way, then toast them to use in colorful sandwiches!

INGREDIENTS

* Sugar cookie dough
* Food color

* 1 egg, separated
* Small paint brushes

WHAT TO DO

Preheat oven to 350 degrees. Use store-bought refrigerated sugar cookie dough, or make your favorite sugar cookie recipe from scratch and chill before using. Gather the kids at the table and roll out dough. Let the kids cut out shapes using cookie cutters or drinking glasses. Mix food coloring in individual bowls, adding a little egg yolk for consistency. Let the kids paint their cookies, using the paint brushes, before they are baked. Glaze with egg white mixed with a little water. Bake for 8 to 10 minutes. Eat!

POTATO PUFFERS

Puff up your baked potatoes with buffet bowls of toppings and provide the kids a whole meal-in-one.

INGREDIENTS

* 8 to 10 large potatoes
* 1 cup soft margarine
* 3 cups grated lowfat cheddar cheese
* 3 cups grated lowfat Jack, Swiss, or mozzarella cheese
* 3 cups lowfat sour cream
* 3 cups chili, beef stew, stroganoff, or spaghetti sauce
* 1 cup crumbled cooked bacon or cubed baked ham
* 1/2 cup chopped green onion
* Grilled mushrooms, chutney, salsa, chopped tomato, baked beans, tuna, sauces, thick soups (optional)

WHAT TO DO

Preheat oven to 400 degrees. Wrap potatoes in foil, pierce with a fork, and bake 1 hour, until tender. Set toppings on the table in separate bowls. Slice open potatoes, squeeze the bottoms to puff the potato flesh up from the skin, and place on individual plates or in small bowls. Let the guests top their Potato Puffers with their choice of toppings.

Serves 8 to 10

PUFFY PEOPLE

Have the guests make clones of themselves that are good enough to eat! Be creative and alter the shapes to suit the party theme.

INGREDIENTS

* 1 batch favorite sugar or gingerbread cookie recipe
* Cookie cutter in shape of a person or other shape
* Decorative candies, such as Red Hots, sprinkles, chocolate chips, raisins
* Tubes of frosting with decorator tips
* 1 quart vanilla or favorite flavor ice cream

WHAT TO DO

Preheat oven to 350 degrees. Prepare cookie dough. On a well-floured board, roll dough out 1/4 inch thick. Cut out figures with cookie cutter. Bake for 8 to 10 minutes, or according to recipe directions. When cool, pass out half the cookies, and set the other cookies aside. Let the kids decorate a cookie in his or her own image, using the candy decorations and tubes of frosting. Remove ice cream from freezer. Slice into 1-inch-thick sheets. Use cookie cutter to cut out ice cream people shapes. Place on plain cookie and top with decorated cookie. Eat immediately, or freeze until firm again.

Makes about 12

SILLY SAILBOATS

Sail these Silly Sailboats down the tummies of your guests when they need a refreshing break.

INGREDIENTS

* 1 (3-ounce) package favorite flavor Jell-O
* 1 (8-ounce) carton plain lowfat yogurt
* 2 cantaloupes or 2 oranges
* 8 thin wooden skewers
* 8 paper squares for sails

WHAT TO DO

Make Jell-O according to package directions. Stir in yogurt and chill for about an hour. When thick but not set, beat at highest speed on mixer until doubled in volume. Cut melons in half and remove seeds. Scoop whipped mixture into centers of melon and chill again. When firm, cut melons in half again. Insert toothpicks into paper sails and stick into melon.

To make mini-boats, cut the tops off of oranges and remove pulp. Fill with Jell-O mixture and set in the refrigerator until firm. Slice oranges carefully in half, then in half again. Set on plates, using a toothpick and small square of paper for a sail. Serve a variety of colored Jell-O for fun, and let the kids decorate their sails.

Makes 8

STUFFED BANANAS

Here's an unusual way to serve a delicious combination. The surprise is inside the peel!

INGREDIENTS

* 4 bananas
* 1/2 cup chocolate chips
* 1/2 cup miniature marshmallows
* 1/2 cup chopped nuts
* Foil

WHAT TO DO

Preheat oven to 350 degrees. Peel one section of the bananas and scoop out their insides. Place the fruit in a bowl and combine with chocolate chips, marshmallows, and nuts. Fill banana shells with equally divided mixture and replace opened peel. Cover each banana with foil and bake for 5 minutes. Remove from oven and take off foil covering. Peel back loose strip, stick in spoon, and serve warm to the kids on individual plates.

Makes 4

DAZZLING DRINKS

CHILDREN'S CHAMPAGNE

Birthday parties are special occasions, so celebrate with a sparkling drink in an elegant champagne glass.

INGREDIENTS

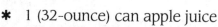

* 1 (32-ounce) can apple juice
* 1 (16-ounce) bottle club soda
* 8 maraschino cherries or strawberries

WHAT TO DO

Combine the apple juice with the club soda and serve in champagne glasses. Drop a cherry or strawberry at the bottom for a special effect, or serve with ice cubes that have fruit imbedded inside.

Serves 8

CHOCOLATE FIZZ

The kids will giggle when they drink this Chocolate Fizz because it tickles as it goes down!

INGREDIENTS

* 4 cups club soda
* 4 cups milk
* 4 tablespoon chocolate syrup

WHAT TO DO

Combine all ingredients in the blender and whirl on high until frothy. Serve in tall glasses with fancy straws.

Serves 8

GLOW DRINK

These drinks are bright and sunny and are sure to give the tummy a special glow.

INGREDIENTS

* 1 (6-ounce) can frozen orange juice concentrate
* 2 cups nonfat milk
* 1 half-gallon orange sherbet

WHAT TO DO

Place the ingredients in the blender and whirl until smooth. (It is best to make these drinks in two batches.) Pour into cups or glasses. Serve with a wide straw and a spoon.

Serves 8

HAWAIIAN HURRICANE

Here's a tropical storm in a glass so hold onto your hats!

INGREDIENTS

* 2 cups crushed pineapple
* 2 cups milk
* 1 pint vanilla ice cream
* 1 tablespoon lemon juice

WHAT TO DO

Combine ingredients in the blender and whirl until smooth.

Serves 4 to 6

MILK 'N' COOKIES SHAKE

Let the kids wash down the birthday cake with a Milk 'n' Cookies Shake!

INGREDIENTS

* 6 (6-ounce) glasses of milk
* 12 favorite cookies, such as black and white sandwich cookies, mint sandwich cookies, peanut butter cookies, or graham crackers, crushed
* 2–3 scoops vanilla ice cream or frozen yogurt
* Blender

WHAT TO DO

Combine the milk, the cookie crumbs, and the ice cream in the blender. Whirl until smooth. (It is best to work in two batches.) Pour and serve with a matching whole cookie.

Serves 6

MONKEY MILKSHAKE

Here's a Monkey Milkshake that's perfect for a party safari!

INGREDIENTS

* 3 cups strawberries
* 3 bananas
* 3 cups milk
* 1 tablespoon vanilla
* 8 to 10 ice cubes

WHAT TO DO

Combine ingredients in the blender and whirl until smooth and fluffy. Serve with straws in fancy glasses.

Serves 4 to 6

PEANUT BUTTER BLITZ

Combine the kid's favorite tastes into this Peanut Butter Blitz!

INGREDIENTS

* 2 cups milk
* 1/2 cup smooth peanut butter
* 1 ripe banana

WHAT TO DO

Place ingredients in the blender and whirl until smooth. Pour into glasses and serve.

Serves 3 to 4

STRAW SUCKER

The "straw" is as much fun as the drink!

INGREDIENTS

* 1 (8-ounce) can frozen lemonade concentrate
* 1 (8-ounce) can frozen grape juice concentrate
* 1 (8-ounce) can frozen orange juice concentrate
* Water
* Licorice whips with hollow centers

WHAT TO DO

Mix all juice concentrates in a large container and add water according to directions on each can. Stir and pour into tall glasses. Cut both ends off hollow licorice to make straws and place in glasses.

Serves 8 to 10

MINI-MEALS

BREAD BOWLER

What fun to eat the goodies inside, and then eat the bowl it comes in!

INGREDIENTS

* 4 small round individual loaves of French bread
* 6 cups of your favorite beef stew, macaroni and cheese, or other casserole dish
* Foil

WHAT TO DO

Preheat oven to 350 degrees. Slice off tops from individual loaves of bread, scoop out insides, and set aside bread for dipping. Fill the loaves with beef stew, macaroni and cheese, or dish of choice. Cover bread with foil and bake for 1 hour. Remove from oven and set on individual plates. Let the guests open the foil, discover the surprise inside the bread, and eat. Share the extra bread for dipping, then tell them to eat the bread "bowls" when they're finished!

Serves 4

BRUNCH-ON-A-STICK

Brunch on a stick? It's fun and easy, and the kids can put it together!

INGREDIENTS

* 1 cup pineapple chunks
* 1 cup strawberries
* 1 cup grapes
* 1 cup banana chunks
* 1 cup apple chunks
* 1 cup cantaloupe chunks
* 8 to 10 brown-and-serve sausage links, cooked and cut into quarters or 2 cups cubed baked ham

* 4 plain or raisin English muffins or bagels, toasted and cut into bite-sized pieces
* Thin wooden skewers
* Melted margarine

WHAT TO DO

Cut up fruit, meat, and bread in chunks or cubes and place in individual serving bowls. Place bowls on counter or table and give each guest a skewer. Let them skewer their food selections, then place them on a broiler pan. Baste with melted margarine and place under broiler for 3 minutes. Turn and broil another 3 minutes until hot and sizzling.

Makes 8 to 10

ELEPHANT EGGS

These aren't really elephant eggs, but don't tell the kids. It's fun to watch these eggs "hatch" at your party.

INGREDIENTS

* 5 eggs
* $1/2$ pound ground turkey sausage
* $1/2$ cup crushed crackers, such as Ritz, saltine, whole wheat, or cheddar (about 20 large crackers)
* Salsa (optional)

WHAT TO DO

Hard cook 4 of the 5 eggs for 15 to 20 minutes. Run cold water over eggs, crack and shell carefully. Divide turkey sausage into 4 portions. Shape each portion into a 4-inch-round patty. Wrap each patty around 1 hard-cooked egg, covering completely. Beat remaining egg in a small bowl. Roll each egg in beaten egg, then roll in crushed crackers. Arrange eggs in shallow baking pan and bake at 375 degrees for 25 to 30 minutes, until sausage is no longer pink. Serve warm or cold, with salsa if desired.

Makes 4

JELL-O CRUNCH

The party guests will be surprised when they find out what gives this Jell-O its crunch. Why not let them try to guess?

INGREDIENTS

* $2 2/3$ cups pretzels
* 1 stick margarine ($1/2$ cup)
* 1 cup sugar
* 1 (8-ounce) package cream cheese, softened
* 1 (9-ounce) container whipped topping
* 2 cups pineapple juice
* 1 (6-ounce) package sugar-free strawberry Jell-O
* 1 (10-ounce) package frozen strawberries

WHAT TO DO

Preheat oven to 400 degrees. Coarsely chop pretzels. Melt margarine and combine with pretzels. Pour into a 9 by 13-inch baking dish and bake for 10 minutes. Remove from oven and allow to cool while you mix the sugar with the cream cheese. Spread the cream cheese mixture over the bottom layer. Spread whipped topping over both layers and chill for 1 hour. Pour the pineapple juice into a saucepan and bring to a boil. Add Jell-O and stir until dissolved. Remove from heat and add frozen strawberries. Allow to partially set in the refrigerator, then spread Jell-O mixture on top of the other layers. Refrigerate 2 more hours, or until set.

Serves 8

PORCUPINE PAT

Serve Porcupine Pat and watch the quills disappear with the veggies!

INGREDIENTS

* Head of cabbage, preferably purple, or lettuce
* Colored toothpicks or thin wooden skewers
* Cherry tomatoes
* Mushrooms
* Bell pepper, cut into squares
* Carrot, cut into rounds
* Celery, cut into large slices
* Zucchini, cut into wheels
* Any other vegetable you like, cut into bite-sized pieces
* Ranch dressing

WHAT TO DO

Cut the bottom off the cabbage or lettuce to make a flat surface and place on a plate. Stick a toothpick into a prepared vegetable, then stick the other end of the toothpick into the cabbage. Repeat, using all the vegetables, and until Porcupine Pat is covered. Let the guests pluck the quills from the porcupine and dip the vegetables into the ranch dressing.

Serves 8 to 10.

QUICKSAND DIP

This Quicksand Dip will have the bread and veggies sinking fast.

INGREDIENTS

* ¹/₂ pound Swiss cheese
* ¹/₂ pound Jack cheese
* 1 ¹/₂ tablespoons cornstarch
* ¹/₂ teaspoon garlic salt
* 1 (12-ounce) can clear soda
* 1 loaf French bread, cut into cubes
* Crackers
* Veggies for dipping
* Fondue forks

WHAT TO DO

Shred the cheeses and place in a large bowl. Add the cornstarch and garlic salt to the cheeses and set aside. Pour soda into a saucepan and heat until the bubbles start to rise. Then slowly add the cheese mixture, stir-ring constantly until all the cheese is melted. Serve with bread cubes, crackers, and veggies.

Serves 8 to 10

SHAPE SANDWICHES

Let the kids create their own geometric designs for the Shape Sandwiches.

INGREDIENTS

* 1 loaf each of bread tinted pink, yellow, green, and blue
* 8 slices ham
* 8 slices bologna or salami
* 8 slices cheddar or American cheese
* 8 slices Swiss or Jack cheese
* Shape cookie cutters or knives

WHAT TO DO

Special order the tinted bread from a bakery in pink, yellow, green, and blue, and have them slice the loaves into thin sandwich slices. Trim off the crust and set out on plates, along with slices of meat and cheese. Let the kids cut out bread, meat, and cheese shapes with the cutters or dull knives. Have them layer their shapes together to make sandwich designs.

Serves 8

CREATIVE CAKES

BLACKBEARD'S TREASURE

Blackbeard's Treasure makes a great centerpiece and is perfect for your shipwreck party, pirate party, or any party. Even the gold doubloons are edible!

INGREDIENTS

* 1 favorite flavor cake mix
* Sheet cake pan (9 × 13-inches)

* Rectangular piece of cardboard covered with gold foil
* 2 cans chocolate frosting
* Assorted colors of frosting tubes with decorator tips
* Chocolate coins in gold foil
* Candies that look like necklaces, bracelets, and other jewelry
* Sheet cake pan

WHAT TO DO

Pour cake batter into sheet cake pan and bake according to package directions. When cool, remove from pan and place on the cardboard covered with gold foil. (Divide the cake in half lengthwise first, if you prefer a double layer cake.) Frost the cake with chocolate frosting.

Clean the sheet cake pan and set it at a right angle to the cake to look like an open chest lid. Frost the pan with chocolate frosting. Decorate the cake using the tubes of frosting to look like a treasure chest. Place chocolate coins and assorted candies on top of the cake.

Serves 8 to 10

CAROUSEL CAKE

This Carousel Cake makes a festive center-piece—and the kids can keep the plastic animals under the big top.

INGREDIENTS

* 1 package favorite flavor cake mix
* 2 cans favorite flavor frosting
* Tubes of frosting with decorator tips
* 1/2 cup brown sugar
* 1 thin red licorice whip
* 8 nonbendable candy-striped straws
* 1 aluminum, plastic, or metal pie pan
* Tiny plastic animals and clowns

WHAT TO DO

Prepare cake mix and bake in two round pans, according to package directions. Frost the top of one cake and place second cake on top; frost top and sides. Make borders of stars, flowers, or other designs around the bottom and top sides of the cake, using the tubes of frosting. Make zigzag lines of frosting on the sides between the borders. Sprinkle brown sugar on the top of the cake to make "sawdust" and place thin red licorice whip in a circle to form a circus ring. Place tiny plastic animals and clowns on the brown sugar. Stick straws around the top edge of the cake to create carousal poles. Place dots of frosting on the tops of the straws. Frost the bottom of a pie pan and set it carefully on the straws, frosting side up, to make a carousel roof. Decorate roof using the tubes of frosting and top with a clown or plastic animal.

Serves 8 to 10

CLOWN CAKES

Let the kids decorate the cakes or make them up ahead of time. Either way, they're sure to delight the hungry crowd.

INGREDIENTS

* 1 package favorite flavor cake mix
* Paper cupcake liners

* 12 ice cream cones
* 1 can vanilla frosting
* Tubes of frosting with decorator tips
* Small candies, such as M&Ms, gumdrops, Red Hots

WHAT TO DO

Prepare cake mix according to package directions and fill cupcake liners half full. Bake and cool. Meanwhile, decorate the ice cream cone with frosting and candies to make the "hats." Remove half the cupcakes from the paper liners. Frost the tops of the cupcakes in the liners and place a plain cupcake upside down on top of each one. Frost the top and sides of the plain cupcake. Decorate the "face" with frosting and small candies. Place the cone hat on top of the cupcake and serve.

Makes 12

CRAZY CUPCAKES

Take a bite of these Crazy Cupcakes and discover the surprise inside!

INGREDIENTS

* 1 package chocolate cake mix
* Paper cupcake liners
* 1 (8-ounce) package cream cheese
* $1/3$ cup sugar
* 1 egg
* 1 (6-ounce) package chocolate chips
* 1 can chocolate frosting
* Tubes of frosting with decorator tips

WHAT TO DO

Preheat oven to 350 degrees. Prepare the chocolate cake batter according to package directions. Fill paper cupcake liners half full. Mix the cream cheese, sugar, and egg together and blend until smooth. Add the chocolate chips to the cream cheese mixture and stir well. Spoon a heaping teaspoonful of the cream cheese mixture in the center of each cupcake. Bake for 25 to 30 minutes, or according to package directions. Frost when cool. (For a special surprise, insert a small toy in each cupcake—but warn the kids to bite carefully!)

Makes 24 cupcakes

DRESSY DOLL CAKE

There's a real doll in this stunning cake, wearing a beautiful ball gown. Although the cake looks intricate and professional, it's surprisingly easy to make. And the birthday star gets to keep the doll when the cake is gone!

INGREDIENTS

* 1 favorite flavor cake mix
* 1 medium-sized round ovenproof bowl
* Vegetable spray
* Paper doily
* 1 small (8-inch) Barbie-type doll
* 2 cans white frosting
* Food coloring
* Tubes of frosting with decorator tips

WHAT TO DO

Prepare cake batter according to package directions. Spray vegetable spray inside the ovenproof bowl and pour in the batter. Bake a little longer than package directions require, testing with a toothpick to see if it's done. Cool, then gently remove cake from bowl, and place it flat side down on a plate covered with a paper doily. Remove clothes from doll and push into top of cake until the doll is submerged to the waist. Cover the cake with frosting tinted a favorite color. Cover the doll's chest completely with frosting, to create a dress and bodice. Then decorate with frosting tubes, to make stars, designs, flowers, or whatever you like. Serve the doll to the birthday guest of honor.

Serves 8 to 10

HAMBURGER CAKE

This giant Hamburger Cake is always the hit of the party! Be sure you make it the centerpiece too.

INGREDIENTS

* 1 package chocolate cake mix
* 1 package yellow cake mix
* 2 cans white frosting
* Food coloring
* Sesame seeds

WHAT TO DO

Prepare chocolate cake batter according to package directions and bake in two round pans. Remove from pans and allow to cool while you bake the yellow cake mix in the two round pans. Remove from pans and allow to cool. Scoop out half a can of frosting and divide it into three bowls. Tint the frosting in one bowl red, in one bowl yellow, and leave one bowl white. Spill the red, yellow, and white frosting over the top of the chocolate cake to look like catsup, mustard, and mayonnaise. Top with the other chocolate cake. Scoop out the remaining half of the frosting and tint it red. Frost the top of the top chocolate cake with the red frosting to simulate tomatoes. Scoop out half of the second can of frosting and tint it green. Frost one side of the yellow cake with green frosting to look like lettuce. You might want to use a leaf tip and press the frosting over the sides of the cake to make the lettuce more visible and authentic looking. Set the chocolate cake on top of the yellow cake covered with the green frosting. Scoop out the remaining frosting and tint it orange. Frost one side of the other yellow cake to make cheese. Place the yellow cake on top of the chocolate cake, frosting side down. Sprinkle sesame seeds on top of the yellow cake to make it look like a sesame seed bun. Serve the Hamburger Cake to the hungry guests.

Serves 10

METEOR SHOWER CAKE

For an outer space look to your party, make this unusual galactic cake, covered with strange chunks of "meteorites."

INGREDIENTS

* 1 premade or 1 package angel food cake mix
* ³/₄ cup sugar
* 3 tablespoons coffee
* 2 tablespoons light corn syrup
* 1 ¹/₂ teaspoons baking soda
* 3 cups prepared whipped cream or Cool Whip, or 3 cups heavy cream whipped with 3 tablespoons sugar and 3 teaspoons vanilla

WHAT TO DO

Bake angel food cake in a tube pan according to package directions. When cool, cut into four layers.

To make the "meteorites," combine the sugar, coffee, and corn syrup in a heavy saucepan, bring to a boil, and cook to hard crack stage (310 degrees). Remove from heat and add the baking soda, stirring until mixture thickens. Don't overbeat. Pour mixture into an ungreased shallow metal pan, but do not spread it out. When cool, remove from pan and chop into small chunks. Cover the cake layers with whipped cream. Decorate with chunks of meteorites. Refrigerate until party time.

Serves 8 to 10

SURPRISE-INSIDE CAKE

Warn the guests there's a surprise inside this curious cake before they take that first bite!

INGREDIENTS

* 1 package favorite flavor cake mix
* A variety of small toys, such as a ball, eraser, cartoon figure, ring, dice, or a variety of small candies
* Extra-small plastic lunch bags
* 1 can favorite flavor frosting
* Tubes of frosting with decorator tips

WHAT TO DO

Bake cake according to package directions in a sheet cake pan (9 × 13-inch) sprayed with vegetable spray. While cake cools, place small toys or candies, enough for all the guests, into small plastic lunch bags and wrap well. While cake is still in pan, lightly score the cake into enough pieces for all the guests, each large enough to fit a toy. Scoop out a small amount of cake from each outlined piece, and insert a wrapped toy into each hole. Repeat until all wrapped toys or candies are in the cake. Flip cake over onto rectangular cake plate and remove cake gently from pan. Frost the cake and decorate using tubes of frosting and tips. Cut and serve cake and watch the surprise on their faces as they discover the secret inside!

Serves 12

ICE CREAM DREAMS

CHOCOLATE PASTA ICE CREAM

Chocolate pasta? Sounds like a silly topping for your ice cream dessert, but it tastes delicioso!

INGREDIENTS

* 1 (12-ounce) package chocolate chips
* 2 tablespoons light corn syrup
* 2 tablespoons margarine
* Waxed paper
* Vegetable spray
* 1 pint favorite flavor ice cream

WHAT TO DO

Melt together chocolate chips, corn syrup, and margarine. Spread waxed paper on a flat surface and lightly spray with vegetable spray. Pour about 1/4 cup of the chocolate mixture onto waxed paper and top with another sheet of waxed paper coated with vegetable spray. With a rolling pin, roll chocolate to 1/8 inch thick. Place on a cookie sheet and set in the refrigerator. Repeat. Remove one chocolate-filled wax paper from refrigerator and set on counter. Peel off top layer and allow chocolate to stand at room temperature for a few minutes. Using a long, sharp knife, slice chocolate into 1/4-inch strips to look like fettucine. Repeat for all layers of chocolate. Place ice cream in individual bowls. Peel strips of chocolate from waxed paper and coil over ice cream.

Serves 4 to 6

CRISPY CRUNCH ICE CREAM PIE

This is only one of many versions of the popular ice cream pie. Use your imagination and make up your own, using your favorite flavors, fillings, and toppings.

INGREDIENTS

* 1 chocolate cookie pie crust, store-bought or homemade using crushed chocolate wafers mixed with melted butter
* 2 flavors of ice cream, crunchy ones preferred
* 1 jar chocolate fudge sauce
* 1 jar caramel sauce
* 1/2 cup chopped nuts
* 1/2 cup chopped crunchy candy bar
* 1 container whipped cream

WHAT TO DO

Set out a carton of ice cream to soften. Spread a thin layer of chocolate sauce over the bottom of the pie crust. Spread softened ice cream on top, filling slightly over half full. Smooth with a knife and place in freezer for about 1 hour. A few minutes before removing pie from freezer, take out other carton of ice cream to soften. Remove pie from the freezer, and spread with a layer of caramel sauce. Sprinkle on nuts and chopped candy bar. Spread the second flavor of ice cream on top, creating a mound. Return to freezer. At serving time, drizzle with remaining chocolate and caramel sauce, which has been slightly warmed in a microwave oven. Top with whipped cream, slice, and serve.

Serves 8

COFFEE CAN ICE CREAM

Let the kids create their own ice cream using a couple of coffee cans!

INGREDIENTS

* 1 cup heavy cream
* 1 cup milk
* 1 beaten egg
* 1/2 cup sugar
* 1 teaspoon vanilla
* Crushed ice
* Rock salt

WHAT TO DO

You'll need two coffee cans—one large and one small—for each pair of kids. Or share the two coffee cans between the group. Combine ingredients except ice and salt and pour into the smaller coffee can. Set the small can into the larger can and fill the space between the two cans with layers of crushed ice and rock salt. Place lids on both cans and roll back and forth between two kids for 10 minutes. Open larger can and pour out the water, salt, and ice. Stir the contents of the inner can. Fill the space between the cans again with layers of crushed ice and rock salt and replace the lids. Roll cans another 5 to 10 minutes. Remove smaller can and scoop out ice cream.

Makes 2 1/2 cups

DIRT AND WORMS

Although it may sound disgusting to you, the kids will love this creepy crawly ice cream dish! And they're in for a big surprise when you start serving the centerpiece that looks like a potted plant!

INGREDIENTS

* 1 half-gallon favorite flavor ice cream, softened
* 1 box chocolate wafer cookies, crushed to a fine powder
* 1 medium plastic flower pot
* Foil

* Gummy Worms
* Plastic flowers with stems to stick into flower pot

WHAT TO DO

Line the flower pot with foil to prevent leakage. Fill three-quarters of the pot with the softened ice cream. Top with the crushed cookies to make the "dirt." Stick some plastic flowers into the center of the pot. Place Gummy Worms in the dirt, some slightly buried, some hanging over the edge of the pot. Remove plastic flowers and freeze the pot of ice cream until serving time. Remove from freezer, replace plastic flowers, and place on the table as a centerpiece without telling the guests that it's dessert. Watch their faces when you begin to dig in—with a trowel?—to serve the cookie crumbs and ice cream! Make sure everyone gets a worm, too!

Serves 8

ICE CREAM CLOWNS

These Ice Cream Clowns look too good to eat! But they're as delicious as they are cute.

INGREDIENTS

* 4 ice cream cones
* 1 pint favorite flavor ice cream
* 4 paper cupcake liners
* Tubes of frosting with decorator tips
* Small candy decorations
* 4 maraschino cherries

WHAT TO DO

Place rounded scoops of ice cream onto the center of paper cupcake liners placed on individual plates. Top ice cream balls with an upside-down cone to make clown hats. Freeze until firm. Decorate one ice cream clown with frosting and candies to look like a clown. Top the cone with a cherry. Put back in the freezer and decorate the remaining ice cream clowns one at a time. Keep in freezer until serving time.

Makes 4

IGLOOS

Serve these individual Igloos that combine the cake and ice cream all-in-one!

INGREDIENTS

* 1 package fluffy white frosting mix
* 4 individual dessert cakes or large brownies
* 1/3 cup fudge, caramel, or strawberry topping
* 1 pint favorite flavor ice cream

WHAT TO DO

Place dessert cakes or brownies on four dessert plates. Spread topping on cake or brownie. Then place one large rounded scoop of ice cream on top. Place all in freezer except one. Quickly frost the "igloo" that was not put in the freezer and then place it in the freezer. Remove another igloo and cover it with frosting. Repeat until all are covered. Freeze for 2 hours.

Makes 4

ORANGE ODDBALLS

Surprise your guests with sweet-stuffed orange shells to give your party a glow!

INGREDIENTS

* 8 oranges
* 1 half-gallon orange sherbet, ice cream, orange Jell-O, or orange cake batter
* 1 tube green decorator frosting

WHAT TO DO

Slice the tops off the oranges and set the tops aside. Remove the insides. If using orange sherbet or ice cream, fill the shells with the softened dessert and set in freezer until firm. If using orange Jell-O, make Jell-O according to package directions, set oranges in cupcake tin for easy handling, and fill oranges with Jell-O. Set in refrigerator until firm. If using cake mix, set oranges in cupcake tin, fill with batter leaving 1/2 inch at the top, and bake according to cupcake directions. When ready, replace orange tops. Make leaves and stem using green frosting tube.

For a variation, scoop out other fruits and fill them with sherbets. Cut a watermelon in half and scoop out fruit. Fill with raspberry sherbet, smooth top to make it look like a watermelon half, and dot with chocolate chips to make seeds. Or fill a hollowed cantaloupe half with orange sherbet and serve to your guests. Try other fruits for fun presentations.

Serves 8

SPIDER WEB PIE

While the guests wonder how you made this amazing Spider Web Pie, you can just say a little fly told you.

INGREDIENTS

* 1 graham cracker pie crust
* 1 quart favorite flavor ice cream, softened
* 1 jar caramel sauce
* 1 quart different flavor ice cream, softened
* Vegetable spray
* 1 large bowl, the diameter of the pie pan
* 2/3 cup sugar
* 1/4 cup water
* Whipped cream

WHAT TO DO

Scoop one flavor of softened ice cream into the bottom of the pie crust. Freeze until firm. Drizzle a layer of caramel sauce over the ice cream, then scoop another flavor of ice cream on top. Shape with a broad knife until smooth. Replace in freezer until firm. Spray vegetable spray around the outside of the inverted bowl. Heat the sugar and water in a heavy saucepan, stirring constantly, until mixture begins to boil. Stop stirring and allow to boil until syrup turns a light golden color. Cool slightly, then pour hot syrup over the bowl slowly, in a thin stream, to create a swirled, open web pattern. Let cool just long enough to allow caramel to firm up and hold its shape. Carefully loosen caramel web from bowl, but don't remove it from the bowl; cool completely in the refrigerator. When ready to serve, remove pie from freezer. Place a large dollop of whipped cream in the center and gently place the caramel spider web on top.

Serves 8 to 10

FAREWELL FAVORS

All good things come to an end—even perfect birthday parties. That's the time to send your guests home with a special "thank-you-for-coming" favor. With a little imagination and creativity, these good-bye gifts can be inexpensive, memorable, and lots of fun. Think about your theme as you explore ideas, or use some of the suggestions that follow. You even can make the favors part of the party fun, by having the kids create their own during activity time!

ANTS-IN-THE-SAND

Here's a whimsical treat the kids will love to eat!

INGREDIENTS

* 2 graham cracker rectangles for each guest
* Chocolate sprinkles
* Sealable plastic sandwich bag for each guest

WHAT TO DO

Place graham crackers in a plastic bag or place between two sheets of waxed paper. Crush with a rolling pin until finely crumbled—until it looks like sand. Divide among the plastic bags. Add $^1/_2$ teaspoon chocolate sprinkles to each bag to make the "ants."

Add other small items, if you want, to make other bugs, such as chocolate chips or raisins for beetles, Red Hots for lady bugs, and Gummy worms for fun!

ART BOX

Pack up some art supplies so the budding artists can continue their creative work at home.

MATERIALS

* Shoe box or other small box for each guest
* Wrapping paper or wall paper samples
* A variety of art materials, such as colored pencils, fancy erasers, a paintbrush, watercolors, crayons or felt-tip pens, glitter, glue, small scissors, a ruler, stencils

WHAT TO DO

Cover the boxes in wrapping paper or the wallpaper samples to make them decorative. Write each guest's name on a box in artistic lettering. Fill the boxes with a variety of inexpensive art supplies, as listed above.

AWARDS AND RIBBONS

Award the guests at the end of the celebration with certificates or ribbons of achievement.

MATERIALS

* Ribbons, store-bought or homemade, in a variety of colors
* Certificates, store-bought from a stationery store or created on a computer
* Permanent felt-tip pens

WHAT TO DO

Award ribbons in a variety of categories of guest behavior, such as the funniest, sweetest, nicest, silliest, and quietest. Or give out awards for game-playing or accomplishments at the party. Pin the ribbons on the kids' clothes and hand them certificates in a short awards ceremony at the end of the party.

BAKER'S CLAY JEWELRY

The kids can wear their favors home when it's jewelry made from Baker's Clay.

INGREDIENTS

* 4 cups flour
* 1 cup salt
* 1 $3/4$ cups water
* Food coloring (optional)

WHAT TO DO

Combine ingredients and knead into dough. Color the dough with food coloring if desired, or leave it plain and let the kids paint their creations after baking. Divide the dough among the kids. Let them form small beads to thread for necklaces or bracelets, or make rings, earrings, or pins. Poke threading holes in beads. Bake at 250 degrees for 30 to 60 minutes, depending on the size of the items. Let the guests finish assembling the jewelry and have them wear their new accessories home.

BAKER'S CLAY PICTURE FRAMES

Here's another fun way to use Baker's Clay and make the party memorable.

INGREDIENTS

* 4 cups flour
* 1 cup salt
* 1 3/4 cups water
* Poster or acrylic paints
* Felt squares for each guest

WHAT TO DO

You can make the picture frames ahead of time yourself, or let the kids make them during activity time. Divide the dough among the kids, and have them shape it into picture frames large enough to hold a Polaroid snapshot. You can make the frame a star shape, a traditional oval or square, an alphabet letter, or a free-form shape. Bake the dough at 250 degrees for 1 hour or more, until firm. Allow the frames to cool 15 to 20 minutes. Then paint with poster or acrylic paints. Cut out a piece of felt the size of the frame. Leaving an opening at the top to insert the picture, glue the felt to the back of the frame. Slip a Polaroid snapshot of each guest into his or her frame to send home as a memento of the party.

BEACH FINDS

The beach, lake, or outdoor park provides lots of free fun favors you can send home with the kids.

MATERIALS

* Shells, driftwood, and other items found along the beach
* Beach pail, decorative box, or fancy bag for each child
* Poster or acrylic paint and/or construction paper

WHAT TO DO

If you host your party at the beach, lake, or outdoor park, collect a number of shells or other nature items to send home with the kids. *(Be sure to get permission to take things from the park.)* You also can buy shells and beach items at specialty stores, if you prefer. Let the kids paint the items during the party, or have them create a collage on a sheet of construction paper. Place the items in a box, a sand pail, or a decorative bag with a handle, then let the kids take home their nature finds.

BOATS AND FLOATERS

Here's a wet and wacky favor idea that's perfect for a water theme party.

MATERIALS

* Plastic boats, plastic sand pails, large colorful sponges, plastic action figures, small plastic toys, or a variety of sink-and-float items

WHAT TO DO

If your party has a water theme, give the kids plastic boats or other items that float to take home and enjoy in the bathtub or swimming pool. Or give them plastic sand pails, large colorful sponges, plastic action figures, small plastic toys, or a collection of sink-and-float objects so they can have some creative play in water.

BUBBLE STUFF

Kids love to take home bottles of bubble solution—they provide hours of after-party play.

MATERIALS

* Bubble solution (page 160)
* Small plastic bottle for each guest
* A variety of blower items to use with the bubble solution (page 160)

WHAT TO DO

Pour the homemade bubble solution into plastic bottles. Fill a large bag with a variety of bubble blowers. Have the kids reach into the bag, without looking, and take a bubble blower. Include a copy of the bubble solution recipe on the outside of the plastic container so the kids can make more bubble stuff when they run out of the original supply.

BUG COLLECTION

Here's an edible treat the kids can make to take home and share with the family.

MATERIALS

* Trail mix items, such as cereals, nuts, small fruits, seeds, tiny pretzels
* Waxed paper
* 1 (12-ounce) package chocolate chips, melted
* Spoons
* Small bowl
* Plastic sandwich bag for each guest

WHAT TO DO

Provide the guests with lots of different trail mix items, as suggested above. Give each child a

sheet of waxed paper and have them arrange their trail mix items on the waxed paper, in small designs or mounds. Pass around a small bowl of melted chocolate and a spoon, and have the kids spoon over a small amount of chocolate onto the trail mix to create a variety of crunchy, chocolate "bugs." Let cool, peel from waxed paper, and fill bags with the bugs.

BUNCH OF BOOKS

Golden Books make wonderful, long-lasting, and inexpensive gifts to send home with the kids.

MATERIALS

* A variety of Golden Books to suit the party theme
* A variety of coloring books, fun activity books, sticker books, pop-up books, musical books, miniature books, or paperback versions of classic and best-selling books

WHAT TO DO

When looking for Golden Books, pick out stories that match your party theme for the kids to read, share, and take home. If you like, offer a variety of other books for the kids to enjoy, such as the suggestions listed above.

CAPES AND HATS

It only takes a few minutes and a few dollars to make up a collection of creative costumes for the kids to wear home.

MATERIALS

* 1 yard of white felt or fabric for each guest
* Bias tape or ribbon
* Permanent felt-tip pens or fabric paints
* Hats, gloves, shoes, vests, wigs, and other accessories (available at thrift stores)

WHAT TO DO

Cut yard lengths of felt or fabric for each guest. Hem the ends, and cover with bias tape or fringe by pulling threads along the sides. Sew on a length of bias tape or ribbon on two corners to make the cape ties. Let the kids decorate the capes with permanent felt-tip markers or fabric paints and—viola! The guests become Spider Man, Super Woman, or Colossal Kid! Complete the ensemble with thrift store accessories, such as hats, shoes, and gloves, and send the kids home in character.

COCONUT HEADS

If you're having a party with a Hawaiian or tropical theme, let the kids make their own Coconut Heads during activity time. Pass their creations out as favors when the kids depart.

MATERIALS

* 1 whole coconut for each child
* Permanent felt-tip pens, puffy paints, or acrylic paints

WHAT TO DO

Give each child a whole coconut and point out the two dots on the coconut that form the "eyes." Set out permanent felt-tip pens, puffy paints, or acrylic paints, and let the kids create their own funny faces, using the eyes as a starting point. A coconut makes a great foundation for funny features—the funnier, the better. When the kids are finished, award prizes for the funniest, ugliest, silliest, smartest-looking, most creative, most like its maker, and so on. Make up enough categories to make sure every kid wins an award.

COLOR SHAPES

You can make your own creative color shapes materials using recycled or new soft plastic.

MATERIALS

* Soft plastic recycled from a popped beach ball, air mattress, or other water floating device or buy colored plastic at the plastic, hardware, or fabric store
* Permanent felt-tip pens

WHAT TO DO

Find or buy colored plastic materials in a variety of colors. Have the kids draw shapes or figures on the plastic with permanent felt-tip pens, then cut out the shapes. The kids can use the plastic shapes to create designs, pictures, and collages right on the table—the plastic sticks to most flat surfaces. Send the kids home with a plastic bag full of shapes so they can stick them to the sides of the tub while taking a bath.

COMIC BOOKS

Make your own comic books during activity time and let the kids take home their creations.

MATERIALS

* Store-bought comics
* Funny pages from the newspaper
* Construction paper
* Tape, glue, scissors, stapler

WHAT TO DO

Provide a variety of store-bought comics to inspire the kids to make their own. Then have them assemble a four-page book: fold two sheets of construction paper, one on top of the other, in half and staple in the center to make a "book." The kids can make their comics in a variety of ways. They can draw their own comic story right onto the homemade construction paper book. Or they can cut up squares from other comic books and reassemble them to make new ones. Or pass the books around and have everyone contribute a comic panel to each book.

COMPASS AND TREASURE MAP

When your party adventure comes to an end, send the kids home with another adventure—their own compasses and treasure maps.

MATERIALS

* Inexpensive compass for each guest
* Treasure map for each guest
* Small gift for each guest

WHAT TO DO

Purchase inexpensive compasses at the toy or party store and give one to each guest. Then hand them a map (which you have created earlier) to lead them on a treasure hunt on the way home. You can make each map unique by drawing a path from the party home to each guest's home. Or make the maps all the same, centered on a local park or school. Make the treasure discovery something simple, like a sign that says, "You Found It!," accompanied by a small hidden toy.

DINOSAUR ZOO

Bet the kids won't be too scared to go home with these tiny dinosaurs!

MATERIALS

* A collection of small, plastic dinosaurs
* Bug box, other small box, or large plastic egg for each guest

WHAT TO DO

Buy little plastic dinosaurs in bulk packages at the toy store so you have plenty for each guest. Divide the dinosaurs equally among bug collection boxes (available at the toy or science stores), plastic eggs that come apart in the middle, or small boxes filled with sand so the guests have to hunt for their favors.

EDIBLE JEWELRY

Let the kids make their own edible jewelry during activity time.

MATERIALS

* Ring-like cereals, such as Fruit Loops or Captain Crunch
* Yarn or thin licorice for each child
* Tape

WHAT TO DO

Offer a variety of colorful cereals that have holes in the middle. Give each kid a length of yarn long enough to fit around their heads. Tape one end to make it stiff like the tip of a shoelace. Have the kids thread the cereal onto the yarn to make necklaces. Let them wear the necklaces home—and eat them on the way! Substitute shoelace licorice for yarn if you want the entire necklace to be edible.

FACE PAINTS

Send the kids home with a whole new look on their faces!

MATERIALS

* Store-bought or homemade face paints (page 164)

* ¹/₂ of a Styrofoam egg carton for each guest
* Plastic wrap
* Tape
* Paintbrushes or cotton swabs
* Makeup accessories, such as lipstick, eye liner, and blush

WHAT TO DO

Buy face paints or use the recipe on page 164 to create a collection of face paints for the kids to take home. Put the paints in Styrofoam egg shell containers (cut egg cartons in half to make six-compartment sections.) Cover the paint with plastic wrap and tape the carton closed. Provide cotton swabs, paintbrushes, and other makeup items such as lipstick, eyeliner, and blush to accompany the face paints.

FAKE TATTOOS AND EARRINGS

Here's a favor that will last a week, even if the kids do take a bath!

MATERIALS

* Fake tattoos (available at drug and toy stores) or fine point felt-tip pens
* Fake stud earrings

WHAT TO DO

The toy and drugstores have lots of fake tattoos to choose from, so pick out a variety for your guests. Or have them create their own using fine point felt-tip or colored ink pens. During the party, let the kids decorate themselves or one another with the fake tattoos or colored pens, then give them a pack of tattoos or pens to take home. For added fun, give the kids a magnetic "pierced" earring and let them add a fake stud to their earlobes. Have smelling salts ready for shocked parents.

FALSE FINGERNAILS

If you're having a dress-up, Hollywood, or beauty salon party, provide the kids with fancy false fingernails.

MATERIALS

* 1 to 2 packs false fingernails for each guest (available at the drugstore)
* Nail polish, nail glitter, and nail decals

WHAT TO DO

Provide false fingernails to the kids just before the party is over. Let them glue on their own nails, polish them, decorate them with glitter and decals, and wear them home. If you wish, give an extra supply of nails to each guest to use when the first set falls off.

FAUX JEWELRY

Dress up the kids for the trip home in a variety of baubles and bangles.

MATERIALS

* A variety of jewelry items from the thrift or toy store, such as necklaces, bracelets, rings, earrings, watches, and tiaras
* Small decorative jewelry box for each guest

WHAT TO DO

Visit the thrift or toy store and pick up a variety of baubles and bangles for the kids. You'll find you can gather quite a collection for very little money. Wrap the jewelry up in fancy boxes, then let the kids choose the box they want. Have them unwrap the box before they leave to see the faux jewelry they can wear home.

FREAKY FRISBEES

A Freaky Frisbee makes a great toy to take home from the party.

MATERIALS

* Regular, extra-large, or mini-sized Frisbee for each guest
* Acrylic paints or permanent felt-tip pens

WHAT TO DO

Buy a bunch of plain, inexpensive Frisbees. Let the kids decorate the Frisbees with acrylic paint or permanent felt-tip markers before they play with them. Let them keep their creations when the party is over.

GOLD COINS AND FUNNY MONEY

They may not get rich at the party, but send them home with some funny money just for fun.

MATERIALS

* Play paper money
* Play gold coins or chocolate coins in gold foil
* Fake credit cards, receipt book-lets, blank check book, accounting pads, or toy cash registers

WHAT TO DO

If the games in your party involve play money, save a little extra for the kids to take home. It's fun to play with funny money. Play gold coins and play paper money are available at toy stores at low cost, and are a creative way to let

kids learn about money. You might also give the guests a receipt book, a blank check book, a fake credit card, and a small cash register to go with their new-found cash.

MAGIC CARDS AND TRICKS

These magical favors disappear right before your eyes!

MATERIALS

* A variety of magic tricks
* A deck of cards for each guest
* Magician accessories, such as hats, capes, and wands

WHAT TO DO

Head for the toy or magic store and collect a variety of magic tricks and novelty toys for your guests. Hand them out at activity time, so they can try out their new tricks, then let them take their tricks home. Get each guest a deck of cards, too—miniature, regular-sized, or oversized—and teach them some card tricks to show the family. Finally, provide them all with a couple of magician accessories too, such as a wand, hat, cape, or other item. Then watch them disappear!

MAGNETIC MONSTERS

Have the kids help you make these hideous creatures at activity time, then let them take home their creations.

MATERIALS

* Pom-poms in a variety of sizes and colors
* Felt scraps in a variety of colors
* Tiny wiggly eyes
* Feathers in a variety of colors
* Pipe cleaners in a variety of colors
* Glue
* Magnetic tape

WHAT TO DO

Buy a bunch of colorful pom-poms and felt to match, along with wiggly eyes, feathers, and any other small accessories you like. Have the kids glue the pom-poms onto felt cut into circles or ovals sized to fit the pom-poms. For example, if they are making caterpillars using three pom-poms, cut the felt three pom-poms long and one pom-pom wide. Glue the pom-poms to the felt, add feet, legs, arms, horns, wings, tentacles, and so on using felt scraps or pipe cleaners, and glue on wiggly eyes. Add a stick-on magnetic strip to the back of the felt so the kids can stick the monsters on the refrigerator when they get home.

MAKEUP SET

If the kids want to continue the make-over at home, here's the perfect favor.

MATERIALS

* A variety of makeup items, such as lipstick, blush, powder, eyeliner, eye shadow, mascara, lash curler
* Small makeup bag for each guest

WHAT TO DO

Drop by the drugstore and pick out inexpensive makeup items for the guests, as suggested above. Let the kids make up their faces with the makeup first. When they're finished, place the makeup items in a paper bag and let each guest pick out one item to take home. Offer them a small decorative makeup bag to hold the item.

ME DOLL

Imagine the guests' surprise when they open up the favors and find themselves!

MATERIALS

* Color headshots of each party guest
* 1 yard white cotton fabric for each guest
* Scissors
* Thread and sewing machine (optional) or glue gun
* Polyester batting
* Permanent felt-tip pens

WHAT TO DO

Some time before the party date, collect color headshots of the guests from their parents and have them made into iron-on transfers at the photo store or T-shirt shop. Press the transfers onto the top of a yard of white cotton cloth, leaving enough room at the bottom to create a doll's body. Cut out a doll body shape, using head as a guide. With right sides together, sew or glue around the doll, leaving an opening at the top for stuffing. Fill with batting and sew or glue the opening shut. Add clothing detail using permanent felt-tip pens or acrylic paints, or let the kids do it themselves at activity time.

MERINGUE MONSTERS

Let the kids create their own monster favors to take home—if the creatures last that long.

MATERIALS

* 3 egg whites
* 1 cup sugar
* $^1/_4$ teaspoon salt
* 1 teaspoon vanilla
* Food coloring
* Candy sprinkles
* Plastic sandwich bags

WHAT TO DO

Blend egg whites, sugar, salt, and vanilla in a bowl. Beat until mixture stands in stiff peaks. Spoon into four bowls and tint each bowl of meringue a different color using food coloring. With paper or plastic pastry bags, or just spoons, have the kids create interesting shapes with the meringue. Provide candy sprinkles and other decorations so they can add detail to their fluffy critters. Bake at 300 degrees for 12 to 15 minutes on a cookie sheet covered with brown paper. Remove immediately and allow to cool. Place the meringues in plastic sandwich bags for the guests to bring home.

PASTA NECKLACES

These Pasta Necklaces are colorful, easy-to-make, and edible!

MATERIALS

* Noodles with holes in the center, such as macaroni, shells, alphabet
* Vinegar
* Food coloring
* Paper towels
* Yarn

WHAT TO DO

Soak a variety of noodles with holes in the centers in bowls of food coloring mixed with equal parts vinegar. When the noodles become the color you want, pour off excess food coloring and pour noodles onto paper towels to dry completely. Give the kids a length of yarn that will fit over their heads, and let them string the different noodles together to make a necklace, or bracelet, or maybe even a caterpillar. Let the guests wear their designs home, or nibble them on the way.

PERSONALIZED POPCORN BALLS

Make Personalized Popcorn Balls to look like your guests!

MATERIALS

* 10 cups popped popcorn
* 3/4 cup sugar
* 1/3 cup water
* 1/3 cup light molasses
* 1/8 teaspoon salt
* Food coloring
* Plastic wrap
* Ribbon
* Construction paper, felt-tip pens, or puffy paints

WHAT TO DO

Prepare popcorn and place in a large bowl. In a saucepan, combine sugar, water, molasses, and salt. Bring to a boil, stirring continuously. Reduce the heat to medium and cook until a candy thermometer reaches 250 degrees. Add the food coloring, stir, and pour mixture over the popcorn, stirring gently to coat. Using buttered hands, shape the mixture into balls. Wrap balls in plastic wrap and tie with ribbon. Decorate popcorn heads with paper, pens, or puffy paints, to make the eyes, nose, and mouth. Or make goofy faces or monster heads, if you prefer.

PIRATE LOOT

If your party has a pirate theme or the kids are shipwrecked on an island, how about sending them home with some Pirate Loot?

MATERIALS

* Play gold coins and play money
* Fake jewelry or edible jewelry

* Eye patch and bandana
* Compass and treasure map

WHAT TO DO

Gather a collection of pirate loot, such as the items suggested above. Wrap the loot in the bandanas. Hide the bandanas in the yard or party room. Give the kids a treasure map that you've prepared ahead of time to help them find the hidden loot. Don't forget to make them walk the plank on their way out the door!

POPPERS

Poppers offer a fun surprise for the kids when they get home.

MATERIALS

* Toilet paper rolls or paper towel rolls cut in half for each guest
* Small toys, candies, stickers, gum, popcorn
* Red crepe paper
* Ribbon

WHAT TO DO

Fill each toilet paper roll with small toys, candies, stickers, gum, popcorn, or whatever you like. Wrap the roll in red crepe paper and tie off the ends with ribbon to look like a giant Tootsie Roll. Pass out the Poppers as the kids leave and tell them to open the Poppers at home for a fun surprise.

PUZZLERS

These puzzling favors are easy to figure out once the kids get them home!

MATERIALS

* Picture of each guest
* Poster board
* Scissors
* Felt-tip pen
* Spray adhesive
* Large envelope or small box for each guest

WHAT TO DO

Using the puzzle suggestion in the games section on page 141, make enlarged photocopies of the kids' pictures and mount them on poster board using spray adhesive. Draw on outlines of puzzle pieces on the photos with felt-tip pens. Making one puzzle at a time, cut out and place the pieces in an envelope or small box. Send the surprise puzzles home with the kids to assemble later.

RABBIT-IN-A-HAT

These make cute place markers and table decorations as well as favors.

MATERIALS

* Small nut cups
* 2 marshmallows for each guest
* Toothpicks
* Food coloring

WHAT TO DO

Buy small nut cups at a party or grocery store. Stack two marshmallows in the cup, using a toothpick to secure one to another to make a "rabbit in a hat." Decorate the rabbit's face using a toothpick dipped in food coloring.

RUBBER BUGGIES

Disgusting! Creepy! Ugly! Scary! Perfect to send home with the kids.

MATERIALS

* An assortment of rubber bugs, spiders, snakes, rats, or Gummy worms
* Plastic sandwich bags

WHAT TO DO

Buy a bunch of rubber bugs, spiders, snakes, rats, and other disgusting creatures that are sure to delight the kids. Hide them around the house for the guests to discover and let them keep what they find. Collect the critters into small plastic bags for easy carrying, or just let the kids stuff the little critters into their pockets to surprise Mom or Dad when they get home.

SECRET STASH TRAIL MIX

Here's a little secret the kids can keep in their pockets—until it's all gone!

MATERIALS

* Sealable plastic sandwich bags or decorative cloth bags with a drawstring or Velcro close
* Trail mix

WHAT TO DO

Fill sandwich bags with your favorite trail mix recipe and give them to the kids to stash away in their pockets. Or if you have time, sew up some decorative cloth bags to store the trail mix. Add Velcro or a drawstring to keep the bag closed. After the trail mix is eaten, the bag is a stand-alone gift.

SINGLE CASSETTES

Kids love music, so send them home singing a tune.

MATERIALS

* Cassette tapes of popular songs or stories

WHAT TO DO

Buy inexpensive cassette tapes with the kids' favorite pop hits, or buy the younger guests some stories-on-tape. Provide a variety to choose from and let the kids draw one out of a hat. Or wrap them up and let them be surprised when the favor is opened.

SQUIRT TOYS

If the party falls during a hot spell, or you've got a water theme, give the kids water squirters to enjoy the rest of the day.

MATERIALS

* Water guns, turkey basters, water balloons, plastic catsup bottles, squirt bottles, small buckets

WHAT TO DO

Water guns are the easiest way to get one another wet, but you can also use turkey basters, water balloons, squirt bottles, or any of the above suggestions to send home with the guests.

STAR CARDS

Create an interest in trading cards with this starter set to take home.

MATERIALS

* Packs of trading cards with a theme, such as sports, stars, space, nature, animals
* A small box in which to keep the card collection for each guest

WHAT TO DO

Trading cards aren't limited to sports figures anymore. There are movie star trading cards, outer-space cards, nature cards, animals cards, magic cards, adventure cards, Dungeon and Dragon cards, and just-about-anything cards. Give the kids a few minutes at the end of the party to do some trading before you send them home with their new collections.

SURPRISE BALLS

These balls are fun to open, especially when there's a surprise inside!

MATERIALS

* Crepe paper streamers
* A large supply of small toys
* Tape or stickers

WHAT TO DO

Buy a large supply of small, inexpensive toys, such as stickers, whistles, rings, or gum. Set one item at one end of the crepe paper streamer. Wrap the streamer around the item a couple of times, then lay a second item on the crepe paper, and continue wrapping and adding more items until the streamer is finished and you have a ball full of surprises. Secure the end of the crepe paper with a sticker or tape, and give one to each guest as you say good-bye.

SWIRL STICKS

Here's a colorful gift that will keep the kids moving.

MATERIALS

* Length of wide ribbon or crepe paper streamer for each guest
* Pencil, chopstick, or dowel for each guest
* Tape

WHAT TO DO

Tape lengths of wide ribbon or crepe paper streamers to the end of pencils, chopsticks, or dowels to make the Swirl Sticks. Tell the guests they can wave the colorful streamers around in the air to make fascinating designs.

THRIFT STORE ENSEMBLES

Take a trip to the thrift store in search of perfect outfits for your guests.

MATERIALS

* Thrift store items, such as hats, dresses, shirts, pants, shoes
* Accessories, such as jewelry, gloves, scarves, capes, neckties
* Boxes
* Wrapping paper

WHAT TO DO

Collect a complete ensemble for each guest if you can, including hat, dress or shirt and pants, and shoes. Add a few fun accessories, such as jewelry, gloves, scarves, capes, neckties. Package everything in boxes and wrap with colorful paper. Give one wrapped box of clothes to each guest to take home for dress-up.

TOOTHBRUSH-TO-GO

These toothbrushes make cleaning your teeth a lot more fun.

MATERIALS

* Toothbrushes in a variety of colors
* Puffy paints
* Ribbon

WHAT TO DO

Buy colorful toothbrushes for the guests. Write their names on the brush handles with puffy paints, then decorate with hearts, stars, or other shapes and designs. Tie a ribbon around each toothbrush, along with a fun kids' toothpaste, and pass them out at the end of the party.

VIDEO VIEWING

A home video favor can entertain the guests for hours after the party's over.

MATERIALS

* Inexpensive kids' videos

WHAT TO DO

Many of the discount stores have inexpensive videos you can purchase for your guests to take home. You can select from favorite movies, cartoons, kids' shows, TV reruns, and music videos—all sure to appeal to the kids.

WATER FUN

Gather a collection of water toys to play with in the bath or pool.

MATERIALS

* Bubble bath
* Small carved soaps
* Washcloth critters
* Water squirters
* Plastic boats
* Body paints

* Cartoon washcloth
* Ribbon

WHAT TO DO

Gather a collection of bathtub and kiddy pool toys to send home with the water-lovers. You might include packets of bubble bath, small carved soaps, water squirters, plastic boats, body paints, and other fun water toys. Bundle them up in a cartoon washcloth and tie the corners together with ribbon.

WEIRD CANDY

There's a lot of weird candy on the market today—and the kids love it.

MATERIALS

* A variety of weird, strange, and disgusting looking candy, such as Pond Scum, Pop Rocks, Slime

WHAT TO DO

See if you can gross out the kids with a goody bag full of disgusting candy. They'll love it.

WHISTLES AND TWEETERS

Give the kids noisemakers to take home.

MATERIALS

* Harmonica, kazoo, whistle, or other inexpensive musical instrument or noisemaker

WHAT TO DO

Give the guests some easy and fun-to-play musical instruments or noisemakers, then send them home before they get too loud!

WHITE ELEPHANT GIFTS

Give them something they never asked for, don't want, and wish they didn't have!

MATERIALS

* Ask each guest to bring something from home that they don't want anymore

WHAT TO DO

Have the kids pick out something from home that they don't want anymore. Ask them to wrap it in fancy wrapping paper and bring it to the party. Set the gifts on the table for everyone to see and let each guest choose a wrapped package at the end of the party. After they open up the silly gift, make them take it home!

INDEX